Calculator Power!
Profits in Discounted Notes

© February, 1991, NoteWorthy Investments, Inc.

Note*Worthy* Investments, Inc.

P. O. Box 31451
San Francisco, CA 94131
Voice: (415) 824 1864
Fax: (415) 824 7720
Visit our web site at: www.noteworthyusa.com

Dedicated, with love, to our wives who gave us the support and understanding that helped make this book and our business possible. And to Emily for helpful suggestions. *JR* and *DR*

11th Printing
Fifth Edition, May, 1999

Printed in the United States

First Rights, Published by **Note***Worthy* Investments, Inc.

This book is for instruction only, and is intended to provide accurate information. It is offered with the understanding that the publisher and authors are not engaged in rendering legal, accounting, tax or other professional services to its readers. If legal or other assistance is required, the services of a competent professional should be obtained.

Richards, Jonathan

Calculator Power, Jonathan Richards and Dave Roberts

ISBN 1-885847-03-3

1. Deeds of Trust 2. Mortgages 3. Real Estate Investment

Table of Contents

Introduction

One of the most exciting ways to make money in real estate is not to own real estate at all, but to own the "paper" or notes that secure that real estate. It is actually possible to make a larger profit by investing in discounted notes and mortgages than by investing in the property itself. This workbook will give you insights into how to do this through investing, buying, selling and brokering discounted mortgages and notes.

The problem with making money in discounted mortgages is that it involves some familiarity, even intimacy, with a financial calculator. When talking with would-be investors in discounted notes we have found they had one of two responses to the use of a financial calculator. One response was that glazed over look of boredom and disinterest. The other response was one of fear, bordering on terror, at the idea of dealing with math calculations. Usually that was the end of their interest in discounted notes.

That is very unfortunate as this business has the potential to be extremely profitable and fascinating. Not only is it unfortunate, it is also unnecessary. In fact, far from being boring or fearful, we find that **playing** (we prefer that word to **working**) with the calculator is one of the most interesting and enjoyable aspects of this business. Indeed, we are not afraid to say that we are downright enthusiastic about **playing** with the calculator and continue to be awed and amazed by what it is capable of doing.

Certainly, this note buying and brokering business could not be possible without it. As our fingers *dance* over the keys we use in our calculations, the correct numbers keep appearing as if by magic. We hope this sense of *dancing* on the keys and feeling the wonder of what the calculator can do doesn't leave us.

To work the problems and to understand the concepts you will need (obviously) a financial calculator. This calculator must have the following keys: **N, %i, Pmt, PV and FV**. Both Texas Instruments and Hewlett Packard make fine calculators. Each calculator is different, so we have made no assumptions about your particular model. We must assume you have read the booklet that comes with your machine, and understand its peculiarities. See **Appendix #1** if you are having problems.

For $20 you can buy a calculator that will solve all the problems you will meet in this book and deal with all the discounted notes you will see in the real world. We have given you an introduction to the calculator in the first Part. However, it is important that you understand the conventions used by your particular model. See **Appendix #1**.

The financial calculator is not only *user friendly,* but it has made it possible to craft offers to buy notes that are so deliciously complex that such offers would not have been possible on a large scale before the invention of these marvelous machines.

We have laid out this book so that you will begin immediately to understanding the powerful concepts of the *time value of money.* If you stick with the exercises, a whole new world of financial information will become available to you. We present the same concepts several times in different ways. In this way you will begin to grasp each new idea as you will see it several times.

In the step-by-step approach we use in this book you will not have to worry about getting bored, lost or confused. We have indicated an average amount of time required for each lesson. If you spend about this much time on each lesson you will be able to absorb what you have learned more efficiently. You simply cannot and should not go through the entire book all at once. If you work at the problems in order and give yourself enough time to digest the information, you will truly learn the power of the *time value of money.*

We use a high 20% or more yield on many of the examples because that is the kind of return we can expect in this very lucrative business. We use a large print format because small print makes the subject matter appear dense and more difficult than it is. We want you to fly through this book.

We have indicated answers and solutions without using cents. Because of the rounding used by different machines, you may get trivial differences from our answers. If you are within the dollar amount we indicate, your answer is correct.

Whether you go into the discounted mortgage business or not, the time you spend learning about the *time value of money* concepts outlined in this book will benefit you for the rest of your financial life.

So, let's start the dance, shall we!

Part I:

Back to Basics or How I Learned to Love the Calculator

In this section we will introduce our five financial calculator "friends": N, %i, Pmt, PV, and FV. Once you understand each of these variables in a loan and how to apply them to any given situation, you will be well on your way to enjoying your calculator.

Notes

Chapter 1: Calculating Payments on a Loan

GOAL:

• *At the end of this session you will be able to use your calculator to calculate the payment needed to "amortize" a loan.*

• *You will understand four of the five parameters in any loan:* **N**, **%i**, **Pmt**, **PV**, **FV**. *In Chapter 2 we will use the* **FV** *key.*

• *You will be able to figure annual, semi-annual, quarterly, or monthly payments*

TIME: 25 minutes.

Notes

This beginning section will give you basic information on financial calculators using the standard key strokes for most models. It is assumed that you have read the manual that comes with your calculator and understand how to put the important values into the financial registers.

If you are having trouble getting the correct answers it is probably for one of the following reasons:

• Your particular calculator may require that you put in outgoing payments as a negative number and incoming payments as positive number.

AND/OR

• Your particular calculator may automatically divide the annual per cent interest by 12. You will have to change the number used to divide the interest to coincide with the problem. Consult your manual to see how to do this.

AND/OR

• Your calculator may have *constant memory* and you may not have cleared the registers before doing a new problem. You should always clear any numbers that remain from any previous calculations. Consult your manual to see how to do this.

Now remember, the calculator won't bite, self-destruct, or yell at you if you touch it or even make a mistake. In fact, it is very forgiving (some may even prefer it to most other relationships because of this)!

Refer to **Appendix #1** if you are having problems.

A financial calculator allows the investor to calculate:
- The payment on a fully amortized loan
- The time to amortize a loan
- The present value of a series of payments
- The balloon payment due on a loan
- The remaining balance on a loan
- The interest rate on a loan

By understanding how the calculator can help you work with these problems and discounted notes you will begin to comprehend the power of the *time value of money*.

Calculating the Loan Payment on a Fully Amortized Loan

All financial calculators have 5 unique keys (or registers): **N**, **%i**, **Pmt**, **PV**, and **FV**.

- **(N)** is the total *Number* of equal payments in a loan
- **(%i)** is the *Interest Rate* per payment
- **(Pmt)** is the *Payment* received or paid out each period
- **(PV)** is the *Present Value* or the amount borrowed
- **(FV)** is the *Future Value* after the payment period

MODEL LOAN: You are borrowing $100,000 at 10% interest payable over 30 Years.

To calculate the *monthly* payment on this loan we must put into the registers the three known numbers, viz. **PV** = $100,000, **%i** = 10%, and **N** = 30 years. Since the loan is fully amortizing, there is no need to use **FV** (we will use **FV** later when we play with balloon payments). These are the steps:

1). Clear the Calculator of any other numbers that may be stored in the Financial Registers from previous calculations.

2). You may want to change the display to show only two decimal places in all your calculations. Otherwise, when you are figuring monthly percentages, the figures to the right of the decimal point will go on and on. You'll see. Consult your manual to see how to do this.

3). Put 100000 into the calculator and push **PV**, the amount of the loan. This puts $100,000 into the **PV** Register.

4). To place the interest in the **%i** register you must find what the monthly interest is since we are looking for the monthly payment. Take 10 and divide it by 12 to get the monthly interest. 10 divided by 12 is 0.83. Push the **%i** button. You now have 0.83 in the **%i** register. *(It is important to do the actual calculation. If you merely put .83 in the %i register you will get a slightly wrong answer. The reason is that the calculator carries all the decimals* *internally, and will use them when figuring the answer. If you put in .83 you are putting in an incorrect number. The correct number is .8333333333.)* If your calculator automatically divides the interest by 12 you can skip this division.

5). To place the number of payments in the **N** register, you must find out how many months are needed to amortize the loan. We know it is 30 years, and to find the months we multiply 30 years by 12 months. This gives us 360 months to amortize the loan. Push the **N** button. You now have 360 in the **N** register.

If you could look into the 5 registers you would see these numbers:

N	%i	Pmt	PV	FV
360	.83333	0	100000	0

1.

To calculate the monthly payment to amortize this loan push a compute key or the **Pmt** key depending on your calculator. Your calculator will, with luck, come up with 877.57. This amount will completely *amortize* or pay off a $100,000 loan at 10% annual interest in 30 years.

Now that we have all the figures we need, let's play with this a little.

1). Clear the calculator.

2). Put in the figure for **N** (360) , **%i** (10 ÷ 12= .83333333), and **Pmt** (877.57), and solve for **PV** (It should be 100000).

3). Clear the calculator again and put in the figure for **N** (360), **Pmt** (877.57), and **PV** (100000), and solve for **%i** (It should be .8333333333)

4). Clear the calculator again and put in the figure for **%i** (.83), **Pmt** (877.57) , and **PV** (100000), and solve for **N** (should be 360)

You already solved for **Pmt** up above. The point is that if you know at least three of the numbers, you can solve for the fourth every time. Further, it doesn't even matter what order you use when you put the amounts in. For instance, in (1) above, you can enter the amounts beginning with **N** or **%i** or **Pmt** and follow it in any order at long as all three are entered. Isn't that neat! So let's try some other loans.

---Questions and Challenges---

☞ What would be the *monthly* payment on a $200,000 loan at 9% for 25 Years? PUT THE FOLLOWING VALUES IN EACH REGISTER AS DESCRIBED ABOVE: (Remember your calculator may automatically divide the **%i** by 12 if you put 9 in the **%i** register.)

N	%i	Pmt	PV	FV
300	.75	(?)	200000	0

To calculate the *monthly* payment to amortize this loan push the correct key to compute the Pmt.

2.

Answer: **Pmt** = $1,678.39

☞ Sometimes payments are made quarterly instead of monthly. What would be the *QUARTERLY* payment on a $300 loan at 5% for 3 years? (If your calculator *automatically* divides the **%i** by 12 you will have to change it for this problem to divide the **%i** by 4. Consult your manual to see how to do this.)

N	%i	Pmt	PV	FV
12	1.25	(?)	300	0

Comment: To calculate the *quarterly* payment to amortize this loan push the correct key to compute Pmt.

3.

Answer: Pmt = $27.08 (Now this is a little tricky. You have to divide the interest by 4 instead of 12 and multiply the number of years by 4 instead of 12. Do you see why?)

☞ What would be the *monthly* payment on $5,342,456.78 loan at 7.5% for 27 years?

N	%i	Pmt	PV	FV
324	.63	(?)	5,342,456	0

4.

To calculate the *monthly* payment to amortize this loan push the correct keys to compute Pmt.

Answer: Pmt = $38,504.89

Occasionally you even run across notes where the payments are made only once a year. What would be the *annual* payment on a $10,500 loan at 15.5% amortized over 13 years? We like these because you don't have to divide the interest and multiply by the number of years. (Again, if your calculator automatically divides the %i by 12 you will have to change it to correspond to the problem.)

N	%i	Pmt	PV	FV
		(?)		
				5.

Answer: Pmt = $1,922.88

☞ What would be the *monthly* payment on a $5,500 loan at 9.75% interest amortized over 19 years?

N	%i	Pmt	PV	FV
		(?)		
				6.

Answer: Pmt = $53.10

☞ What would the *semi-annual* payment be on a $75,000 loan at 13.75% amortized over 40 years? (What should you do if your calculator automatically divides the interest by 12?)

N	%i	Pmt	PV	FV
		(?)		
				7.

Answer: **Pmt** = $5,181.62. Remember to multiply **N** by 2 and divide **%i** by 2.

*The most important thing you have learned in this lesson is to make the payment periods (**N**) consistent with the interest (**%i**) and payments (**Pmt**). You should now be comfortable in calculating the payments needed to amortize a loan whether the payments are monthly (as most loans will be) or quarterly, semi-annually or annually.*

"Invest in Inflation. It's the only thing that's going up."
WILL ROGERS

Notes

Chapter 2: Remaining Balance

GOAL:

• *At the end of this session you will be able to use your calculator to calculate the balance due on a loan after several payments have been made.*

• *You will use the* **PV** *key to find the balance due, and*

• *You will now get a chance to use the* **FV** *key as another way to find the balance due*

TIME: 17 minutes.

Notes

Often when a note is offered to you, several payments have already been made on the loan. The *remaining balance,* after a certain number of payments have been received, can be calculated in three ways on most financial calculators.

How to Find the Balance Due

Method #1: (Using "BAL" Key.) There may be a "balance" or "bal" key on your calculator. You simply key in number of payments that have been made and then press the "bal" key. The answer shown in the window is the balance left to be amortized or paid off. Consult your calculator manual on how to find the *balance due* using the "bal" key.

Method #2: (Using PV Key.) You can use the familiar **N**, **%i**, **Pmt**, **PV** and **FV** keys to find the remaining balance. Key in the regular note as you ordinarily would, then put in the amount of payments that remain to be paid and calculate **PV**. (This method is not as accurate as method #1, but is sufficient for our purposes.)

We have a $60,000 note amortized over 10 years at 11.5% interest. What is the balance after 5 monthly payments have been made?

N	%i	Pmt	PV	FV
120	.96	(?)	60000	0

Comment: Calculate the current payment. Remember we must first solve for the missing variable before going on. In this case, it is **Pmt**.

8.

Answer: Pmt = $843.57. This is an 11.5% loan amortized over 10 years. What is the amount due after 5 payments have been made? Again, remember to divide **%i** by 12, multiply **N** by 12. Soon this will be second nature to you.

We subtract 5 from the **N** of 120 to get 115 and re calculate **PV**.

N	%i	Pmt	PV	FV
115	.96	843.57	(?)	0

9.

Answer: PV = $58,631 due after 5 payments have been made. What if you had bought the above note, and the payor decided to pay off early, after only 25 payments had been made? What would the balance on the note be then?

N	%i	Pmt	PV	FV
(95)			(?)	

Comment: How many payments are there left? That goes under N.

10.

Answer: PV = $52,453.

After 119 payments have been made?

N	%i	Pmt	PV	FV
(1)			**(?)**	

Comment: That's right, there is only one payment left to go.

11.

Answer: **PV** = $835.57. This is the balance when there is only one payment left to make.

Method #3: (Using FV Key.) You can use the **FV** key in a similar manner to find the balance due on a loan. (This method is not as accurate as method #1.) However, in this case you will put the number of payments received in the **N** register (remember in **Method #2** we put the number of payments *left,* i.e., not yet *received*) and calculate **FV**. We have a $60,000 note amortized over 10 years at 11.5%.

N	%i	Pmt	PV	FV
120	.96	**843.57**	60000	0

Comment: This is the original 11.5% loan amortized over 10 years.

12.

To find out the balance due after 5 payments have been received simply put 5 in the **N** Register and calculate **FV**.

N	%i	Pmt	PV	FV
5	.96	**843.57**	60000	(?)

13.

Answer: FV = $58,631. The balance due after five payments have been received is $58,631. This is the same answer we calculated above when using the **PV** key (Box #9). In other words, you can use **PV** to figure the amount when you know how many payments are left, or use **FV** to figure the amount when you know how many payments have been made.

--- Questions and Challenges ---

☛ Your Aunt Harriet (who has *lots* of notes) has a $12,000 note amortized over 12 years with 13.5% interest, and monthly payments of $168.69. She asks you to calculate the balance due after 12 payments have been paid:

Method #1: Solve for **PV**

N	%i	Pmt	PV	FV
			(?)	

14.

Answer: **PV**= $11,569.

Method #2: Solve for **FV**

N	%i	Pmt	PV	FV
				(?)

15.

Answer: **FV**= $11,569.

☛ What is the balance after 140 payments have been made?

Method #1: Solve for **PV**

N	%i	Pmt	PV	FV
			(?)	
				16.

Answer: **PV** =$656.

Method #2: Solve for **FV**

N	%i	Pmt	PV	FV
				(?)
				17.

Answer: **FV** =$656.

*You now understand how to calculate the balance remaining on a loan after a certain number of payments have been made. You have seen how the **PV** and **FV** registers work on the calculator. What's really important to keep in mind is that each time a payment is made on an amortizing loan the balance due on the loan is reduced. This is important to know, since many notes will come to you "seasoned," meaning the payor has been making payments on the note for months or even years. Usually the person selling the note won't know the Present Value or Balance Due of the note (on fully amortizing loans, the Present Value will always be lower than the*

Original Value and will be considerably lower if several years have gone by). They may think it is still the Face Value or Original Value of the note. By calculating the Present Value, you will be able to show the note seller what the Balance Due to him or her is NOW. Therefore, the discount offer you make may not appear so steep.

"Hard work is the yeast that makes the dough rise."

Notes

Chapter 3: Balloon Payments

GOAL:

• *At the end of this session you will understand balloon payments and how both the balloon and the regular payments are calculated.*

• *You will understand that the payment on a loan may fully amortize the loan so there is no balloon payment, or*

2nd most common

• *The payment may only cover the interest on the loan, so the balloon payment will be for the entire amount of the loan, or*

most common

• *The payment may be fully amortizing over a certain number of years, but with a balloon due in fewer years, or*

• *The payment may not even cover the interest or the principal, so the Balance Due keeps growing each month. This is called a Negative Amortization Loan.*

TIME: 23 minutes.

Notes

What about partial balloons?

For instance: $50,000 loan amortized over 30 years at 9.5% interest: pmts of! $420.10/mo

with a partial balloon ~~every 24 years!~~ or principle paydown needed after every 4 years (i.e., a % balloon after every few years).

Many notes have not only monthly payments, but also have balloon or large payments due after a certain period of time. A common note is written with interest only payments, then a balloon is due for the principal amount. For example, if you borrowed $50,000 and were making interest only payments every month at 12% you would owe $500 per month. ($50,000 X .12 = $6,000 interest only per year. Divide $6,000 by 12 months. Your payments are $500 per month.) However, you still owe the principal amount of $50,000. This will come due at some future time as a balloon payment. Since the balloon is calculated using the **FV** key, we will get a chance to play with **FV**.

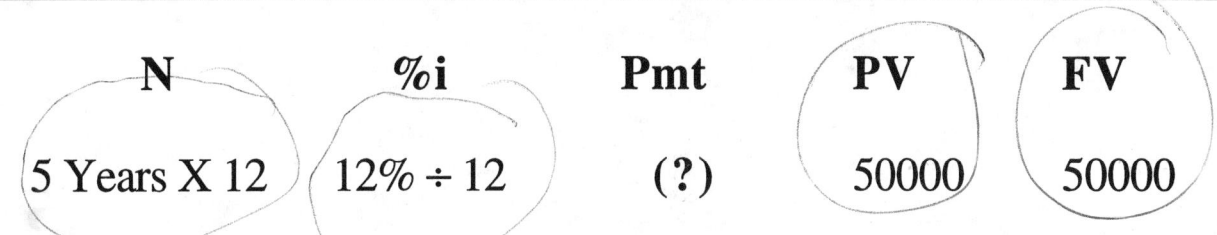

N	%i	Pmt	PV	FV
5 Years X 12	12% ÷ 12	(?)	50000	50000

Comment: We are figuring the payment with a **PV** of $50,000 and an **FV** of $50,000.

18.

Answer: Pmt = $500. In five years we will owe a balloon payment of $50,000. (We could have gotten the same answer by multiplying $50,000 by 12% to find the annual interest owed, and then dividing that by 12 months to get a $500 per month payment.) You will notice that with interest only loans the monthly payment is always the same regardless of the number of months (**N**) left on the loan. With amortizing loans, the monthly payment on the same present value is changed as the length of the note changes (**N**); this is true since the amount necessary each month to pay off the loan varies greatly depending on how long it takes to pay it off.

---Questions and Challenges---

☛ What is the balloon due on a $3,000 loan, at 12%, with payments of $30 per month all due in 60 months?

N	%i	Pmt	PV	FV
60	12 ÷ 12=1%	30	3000	(?)

19.

Answer: FV = $3,000. That was pretty simple, we hope!

☛ What is the balloon due on the above $3,000 loan, at 12%, with payments of $30 per month all due in 120 months?

N	%i	Pmt	PV	FV
(120)				(?)

20.

Answer: **FV** = $3,000

☛ What is the balloon due on the above $3,000 loan, at 12%, with payments of $30 per month all due in 10,000 months?

N	%i	Pmt	PV	FV
(10000)				(?)
				21.

Answer: FV = $3,000. Why is the balloon the same no matter how many payments are made? Because the $30 per month only pays the 12% annual interest, it does not pay down (amortize) the loan. (It doesn't matter how long the loan is for.)

☛ Now the above note is fairly easy to figure, but suppose we get a note like this: what is the balloon on a $10,000 note *amortized* over 30 years, at 14.5% payable monthly, all due in 5 years. (Hint: Now this calculation gets a little more complicated, but is also more magical and fun! First figure the fully amortized note and solve for **Pmt**, then figure the balloon, by changing the **N** to 60.)

Part 1: Calculate the Amortizing Part of the Note

N	%i	Pmt	PV	FV
360	1.2	(?)	10000	0
				22.

Answer: First part: **Pmt** = $122.46. Great! Now change **N** to 60 and solve for **FV**. You're figuring how much will still be owed on the note after 5 years have gone by (which is the same as saying what will the balloon be at that time).

Part 2: Calculate the Balance Due:

N	%i	Pmt	PV	FV
				(?)
				23.

Answer: 2nd Part: **FV** = $9,858. Good! You have figured the balloon due on a $10,000 loan at 14.5% interest amortized over 30 years but all due in 5 years.

☛ Great! Let's try one more. Your rich Aunt Harriet has a balloon payment due on a $46,000, 3 year note at 12% annual interest, with annual payments of $4,754.05. What is the balloon payment? (Remember that with annual payments we don't have to divided **%i** by 12 or multiply **N** by 12.)

N	%i	Pmt	PV	FV
				(?)
				24.

Answer: **FV** = $48,584. (Note: This is a negative amortization loan, because the Balloon or **FV** is larger than the amount borrowed. In other words, the monthly payments weren't even enough to cover the interest owed on the note. So the unpaid interest accumulated and was added to the original amount of the note.)

Aunt Harriet has a note that is *increasing* in value. She really knows how to write the terms on a note!

*You should be very comfortable figuring balloon payments and using the **FV** key. You have worked with interest only loans, fully amortizing, partially amortizing, and fully amortizing loans over X years but due in Y years with a balloon payment. It's amazing how many ways there are to structure a note, isn't it?*

✗ Question: In what situations are negative amortization mortgages used? Why only pay part of the interest only payments?

Chapter 4: Present Value

GOAL:

• At the end of this session you will be able to figure the value TODAY of a lump sum of cash you will receive in the future

• You will begin to understand the importance of "yield" when calculating the Present Value of a sum of money.

• You will see that money to be received far in the future loses its value very quickly

• This, and the next four lessons, present the most important concepts in dealing with discounted notes.

TIME: 23 minutes.

Notes

The idea of **Present** and **Future Value** is merely a way to clearly show you what you probably know intuitively: there is a *time value* associated with money. Besides the risk involved, the *promise* of $1.00 ten years from now is just not worth $1.00 today. That is because the $1.00 available now could be put in the bank or invested at some rate of return. That *rate of return* or *yield* will differ from investor to investor. If you are very conservative you may require a yield of only 7% and consequently, a low risk (and a low profit). If you can handle risk, or have some ability to increase your money, you may require a 20% or higher yield. Your *yield* will depend on your ability to invest and your tolerance for risk.

So let's begin simply. What would you do if someone gave you a choice of receiving $100 now or $100 in 5 years. It's obvious, isn't it? You'd take the money now. However, what if someone gave you a choice of $100 now or $200 in 60 months (5 years?) Let's get out our trusty calculator and figure this out.

N	%i	Pmt	PV	FV
60	(?)	0	100	200

Comment: There are no payments so **Pmt** is 0. You put 100 under **PV** to see what interest rate it would take to have $200 in 5 years.

25.

Answer: **%i** = 13.94%. (Remember on some calculators you will need to multiply your answer by 12.) So if you can make more than 13.94% on your money, which do you choose? That's right! If you take the $100 and invest it at 14% or higher, you will have more than $200 in 5 years.

Single Payment Note

If we were to offer you $10,000 in five years (**FV**), and you needed a 7% yield (**%i**), what would you pay *today* (**PV**) for that single amount?

N	%i	Pmt	PV	FV
5 Years	7 %	0	(?)	10,000

Comment: You must solve for **PV**. You do not need to divide the interest by 12 nor multiply the **N** by 12 because the question is framed in terms of years. Furthermore, the **Pmt** would be 0, because there is only the one payment in five years.

26.

Answer: **PV** = $7,129. The **Present Value** of $10,000 in 5 years is $7,129 because you could invest $7,129 at 7% and get $10,000 in 5 years. Theoretically, it would not matter whether you took the

$7,129 today or the $10,000 in 5 years. They are financially or mathematically the same if you are happy with 7% per annum.

Lottery Example:

Let's figure the **PV** of a series of payments by looking at lottery winnings. Let's say a woman wins a $10,000,000 lottery. The state will pay her monthly over 20 years. The woman comes to you and says she wants to sell her payments because she wants cash now. You make her an offer based on an 18% yield to you. What is the **Present Value** of this lottery prize based on the discount?

N	%i	Pmt	PV	FV
20 years X 12	18% ÷ 12	$\dfrac{10000000}{240}$	(?)	0

Comment: To find the **Pmt** you must divide $10,000,000 by 240 months, because that is the payment you will receive each month.

27.

Answer: PV = $2,699,822. This is a great example of the *time value of money.* Because the payments are taking 20 years to get to you, at your 18% yield you can only pay $2,699,822 for what *appears* to be a $10,000,000 lottery winning.

That is a 73% discount off face value.

--- Questions and Challenges ---

☛ You have an inheritance of $300,000; however, your very rich, but stingy Aunt Harriet won't let you have it for 20 years. If you could somehow work out a deal with her to take a lesser amount today (this might appeal to her miserliness), how much would you need if you could invest it in real estate and get an 18% annual return? *(Don't divide the %**i** by 12, nor multiply the **N** by 12 since the question is framed in terms of years not months.)*

N	%i	Pmt	PV	FV
20	18%		(?)	

28.

Answer: PV = $10,951. (Now wouldn't she go for this amount!) Think of that, you could invest only $11,000 now and have $300,000 in 20 years.

☛ You have a property that is worth $250,000 and you receive an offer for $350,000 but with no payments for 12 years. Is this a good deal? What are you really selling the property for if you can safely invest your money at 9% per year? *(Don't divide the %**i** by 12, nor* *multiply the N by 12 since the question is framed in terms of years not months.)*

N	%i	Pmt	PV	FV
			(?)	
				29.

Answer: **PV** = $124,437. You are really selling your $250,000 property for $124,437 in today's dollars.

☞ Instead of accepting the above offer, you sold the property for $250,000 NOW and invested it at 9% compounded monthly for 12 years. How much would you have? *(NOW you must divide the %i by 12, and multiply the N by 12 since the question is framed in terms of months not years.)*

N	%i	Pmt	PV	FV
				(?)
				30.

Answer: FV = $733,209! Your investment would grow to $733,209 in 12 years. That's why you need to learn how to use a financial calculator. What sounds like a good deal many times will not stand up to your analysis.

☛What is the **Present Value** of $12,000 to be received in 5 years if your yield is 12%? *(Don't divide the **%i** by 12, nor multiply the **N** by 12 since the question is framed in terms of years not months.)*

N	%i	Pmt	PV	FV
			(?)	
				31.

Answer: **PV** = $6,809.

☛ What is the **Present Value** of $1,000,000 in 35 years if your yield is 20%?

N	%i	Pmt	PV	FV
			(?)	
				32.

Answer: **PV** = $1,693. It's amazing but correct!

*You have now made several calculations figuring both the **Present Value** of a payment to be made in the future and a series of payments. You are an expert on **Present Value** calculations, and you now know that a million dollars to be paid to you in 35 years is not worth very much. Most importantly, you have a clear sense of the "time value of money" and how inflation eats into your future earnings and retirement income. You also understand the expression "in today's dollars" that is used often by economists. Now, with the skill you have acquired in using the calculator, you not only can make wise offers on notes, but you can also better project your own personal financial situation.*

"What you think of me is none of my business."

Notes

Chapter 5: Present Value of a Series of Payments

GOAL:

• *At the end of this session you will be able to figure the value TODAY of a series of regular payments.*

• *You will, again, see the importance of "yield" when calculating the Present Value of an income stream.*

TIME: 23 minutes.

Notes

$\mathbf{Y}$ou can use your calculator to find the **Present Value** of several regular payments.

If we were to offer you $100 per month for the next 10 years and you could safely earn 10% compounded monthly on your money what would the **Present Value** of these payments be?

N	%i	Pmt	PV	FV
10 Years X 12	10% ÷ 12	$100	(?)	0

Comment: We are looking for the **Present Value** of a series of regular payments. Future Value is zero because after we had received all the payments there would be no more money paid out.

33.

Answer: PV = $7,567. The **Present Value** of 120 monthly payment is $7,567 because you could invest $7,567 at 10% and get $100 per month for 120 months. Theoretically, it would not matter whether you bought something and paid $7,567 in a lump sum or paid $100 per month for it for 120 months. These two choices are financially the same.

☛ You are selling your investment house for "No Money Down" and carrying back a loan from the buyer for $250,000 at 10% per year amortized over 360 months. You can earn 22% on your money by buying discounted notes. What are you really selling your property for. (Hint: This is a two step process.)

Step # 1: Calculate the payment you will receive each month:

N	%i	Pmt	PV	FV
30 years X 12	10% ÷ 12	(?)	$250,000	0

34.

Answer: Pmt = $2,193. You will receive 360 monthly payments of $2,193, and will be earning 10% annual interest. How much is that income stream worth if you can earn 22% by investing in discounted notes?

Step # 2: Calculate the Present Value of that Income Stream:

N	%i	Pmt	PV	FV
360	1.83	2193	(?)	0

35.

Answer: PV = $119,496. Because you can earn a 22% return (or 1.83% per month) you are really selling your home, in present dollars, for only $119,496, not the $250,000 you thought is was selling for. You can see why knowing about the **Present Value** of money is a very important concept.

---Questions and Challenges---

☞ You are selling your investment house for "No Money Down" and carrying back a loan from the buyer for $150,000 at 11% per year amortized over 240 months. What are you selling the above house for if you could earn 14% on your money? (Hint: First calculate the payments then find the **PV** of those payments at your yield.)

Step # 1: Original Loan.

N=240   %i 11÷12   **Pmt**   PV 150,000.00 **FV**
                                            (?)

36.

Answer: Pmt = $1,548.28

Step # 2: PV of that Loan at your yield of 14%.

N   **%i**   **Pmt**   **PV**   **FV**

                                            (?)

37.

Answer: PV = $124,507.

☞What are you selling the above house for if you could earn 12% on your money?

N	%i	Pmt	PV	FV
240	12÷12=1	1548.28	(?)	
				38.

Answer: PV = $140,614.

You are now an expert on figuring the present value of a series of payments. You can now calculate the Present Value of $100 per month for the next 60 months. You can also see why it is not necessarily a great deal to sell a house for no money down or only 10% down and then carry the note yourself to get a higher selling price. In other words, if you have a way to invest your money at a reasonable interest rate, given the "time value of money," you are much better off to lower the price, and have the buyer get bank financing and get all your money now. This is also a great selling point to get sellers to accept a discount now. This is because you understand that any cash flow has a Present Value depending on the Yield you can get on your money.

"People who know *how*, work for people who know *why*."

Chapter 6:
Future Value

GOAL:

• *At the end of this session you will be able to calculate the Future Value of a sum of money, made on an investment today.*

• *This lesson will reinforce the concepts of "yield" and "time" when dealing with investments.*

• *You will have a better understanding of Inflation and Appreciation.*

• *You will graphically see that compound interest is truly the "eighth wonder of the world".*

TIME: 12 minutes.

Notes

When would I want to figure out FV of a lump sum today (i.e. savings)

When would I want to figure out PV of a series of payments (i.e. saving for retirement, college, vacation, emergency $).

Your calculator can find the compounded **Future Value** of a sum of money invested today. This is the reverse of finding the **Present Value** of a lump sum you will receive in the future. For example, we use **Future Value** calculations when we figure appreciation, or the growth of a sum of money invested now.

Remember your very rich, but stingy Aunt Harriet? Suppose she tells you she is going to give you $100,000 when she dies. Great! However, what if that isn't for several years. What good does that do you now! Well, she says she is going to put it into a trust account at 12% compounded monthly. As you begin to calculate your future wealth at her demise, you think, "How much will I have in 5 years?"

N	%i	Pmt	PV	FV
60	1	0	100000	(?)

39.

Answer: **FV** = $181,669.

However, we know only the good die young. So what would you have if you had to wait 20 years to get your hands on this trust?

Answer: **FV** = $1,089,255. Wow, You only hope you're still able to enjoy it!

☛**Another example**: If we were to offer you $7,129 today and you could invest that at 7% annual interest, what would you have in 5 years? Since the money is compounding, you will receive interest on the interest you received in the previous year. So, let's play with our calculator to figure the **Future Value**.

N	%i	Pmt	PV	FV
5 Years	7%	$0	$7,129	(?)

Comment: You must solve for **FV**. You do not need to divide the interest by 12 nor multiply the **N** by 12 because the question is framed in terms of years.

40.

Answer: FV = $10,000. *If you get an answer close to $10,000 that is sufficient and correct.* The Future Value of $7,129 in 5 years is $10,000 because you could invest $7,129 at 7% and get $10,000 in 5 years. Theoretically, it would not matter whether you took the $7,129 today or the $10,000 in 5 years. They are financially or mathematically the same.

☛If you bought a home for $350,000 (it must be in California) and were expecting inflation to be 5% per year and you were going to sell the house in 7 years, what do you think the selling price will be?

N	%i	Pmt	PV	FV
7 Years	5%	$0	**$350,000**	**(?)**

Comment: The house will go up in value 5% a year so the first year it will go up by 5% or $17,500. So your house will be worth $367,500 at the end of year one. It will go up another 5% in year two, but this is 5% of the new price of $367,500. It will go up $18,375 in year two to a value of $385,875. The calculator does all this work for us for all five years.

41.

Answer: FV = $492,485. The $350,000 house should be worth $492,485 in 7 years assuming it goes up in value 5% each year. That is the beauty of compound interest.

☞The current cost of a 4 year college education is about $45,000 at a public university. You suddenly realize your 6 year old child is brilliant and is going to want to go to a university in 12 years. If you predict inflation will be 7% per year, how much will that college education cost when your child is 18 years old? How much must you invest now at 9% to have that lump sum for your child's college when she is 18 years old?   ∅ FV= 73,652.29

ANSWER: This is a little more complicated, but with your calculator, it's a "piece of cake." We have to divide this into two parts: **1).**

What will the college cost of $45,000 (**PV**) today cost in 12 years (**FV**)? **2).** How much must we invest now (**PV**) to have this amount (**FV**) in 12 years (**N**) at 9% interest (**%i**)?

Part 1: What is the future value of $45,000 if you expect college tuition to go up 7% per year for the next 12 years until your child is 18?

N	%i	Pmt	PV	FV
12 years	7% inflation	$0	**$45,000**	(?)

Comment: We are looking for the college tuition in 12 years (**FV**) at 7% (**%i**) inflation.

42.

Answer: **FV** = $101,348. You will have to pay $101,348 for your daughter to go to college when she is 18 years old in 12 more years. You can see the power of compound interest. What costs only $45,000 today will cost $101,348 in 12 years. If a gallon of gas costs $1.50 per gallon today, what it will it cost when your daughter goes to college? The cost is $3.38 per gallon, so better not buy her that car! If you make $60,000 per year, what must you make in 12 years to maintain your same buying power? The answer is: $135,131, which is why you need to get into the note business if you want any chance of retiring early!

Part 2: What is the present value of that sum of $101,348 if it is invested at 9% so it will grow to the amount needed to meet the tuition payment?

N	%i	Pmt	PV	FV
12	9	0	(?)	101348

Comment: Now you know the **FV** is $101,348. Just change **%i** to 9. If we need $101,348 in twelve years and can earn 9% annual interest, what amount will grow to $101,348 in 12 years?

43.

Answer: PV = $36,032. If we put a one-time deposit of $36,032 in an investment that pays 9% annual interest, it will grow to the amount need for tuition: $101,348 in 12 years. If only we had $36,032 to invest. We'll deal with how to work around that in the next chapter.

--- Questions and Challenges---

☛Suppose you took $25 and invested it for 120 years at 10% compounded monthly, (you're probably thinking, "Why would anyone do such a thing?", but just humor us and go along). How much would your great grandchildren have at the end of that time?

N	%i	Pmt	PV	FV
				(?)
				44.

Answer: **FV** = $3,871,497. Think of how kindly your great grandchildren are going to remember you! Of course, if inflation was running at 6%, a $3 hamburger will cost $3,264 in 120 years!

☛ If my grandfather invested $1 in a **Honus Wagner** baseball card in 1933, and that card went up an average of 25% per year what would it be worth in 1995?

N	%i	Pmt	PV	FV
				(?)
				45.

Answer: **FV** = $1,019,578. And you threw that card away!

☛ I can invest my money at 13.94% compounded monthly. If I invest a certain amount of money, how much will I have after 60 months?

N	%i	Pmt	PV	FV
				(?)
				46.

Answer: You will double your money. Put $5 in **PV** and calculate **FV**. It will equal $10. Or put $3000 in **PV** and **FV** will calculate out to about $6,000. (See box #25)

INTERESTING FACT: Then there is the *rule of 72*. Divide any interest rate into 72 and you can get the approximate amount of time it will take to double your money. In the above example, divide

13.94 into 72 and you get a little over 5 which is why it doubled in 5 years.

*You are now an expert on figuring **Future Value**. You know that a sum of money, earning compound interest, will grow dramatically. You now see the profound effects of inflation and appreciation. Now here comes a critical point. You start thinking about all the investments you should have done or did and wish you hadn't and how much money you would have had today if only....* **DON'T THINK ABOUT IT!**

"Put all your eggs in one basket, and watch the basket."
MARK TWAIN

Chapter 7:

Compounding a Series of Equal Payments (Annuities)

GOAL:

• *At the end of this session you will be able to calculate the Future Value of a series of payments.*

• *This lesson, like the previous lesson, will reinforce the concepts of "yield" and "time" when dealing with investments.*

• *You will understand how to "save" now for a future lump sum.*

• *You will learn to manipulate %i, to get a specific lump sum, or to change the N, to get a payment you can afford in order to save a specific amount.*

TIME: 19 minutes.

Notes

When would I want to find use PV. of a serious of monthly payments? i.e. (if I need to find out how much to invest today to receive a certain amount of income each year).

As we did in the **Present Value** calculations, you can find out the **Future Value** of a series of payments. For example, if you need to accumulate $5,000 in 3 years, and could earn 5.5% compounded monthly in the bank on your money, how much would you need to put in the bank each month?

N	%i	Pmt	PV	FV
3 Years X 12	5.5% ÷ 12	(?)	0	5000

Comment: We are not concerned with the present value, since we are putting away *monthly* payments and want to accumulate $5,000 in 3 years.

47.

Answer: Pmt = $128.06. If you put $128.06 in your bank account every month and earn 5.5% annual interest (compounded monthly) you will have $5,000 after three years.

Future Value computations are useful for calculating the effects of inflation. For example what would a $3 hamburger cost in 5 years if you expect 10% annual inflation? The answer is $4.83. (Did you remember that the answer is framed in years so you don't have to divide the **%i** by 12) What will that hamburger cost in 50 years? The answer is $352.17.

--- Questions and Challenges---

☛ If you need $10,000 in 4 years and could earn 6% compounded monthly, how much would you have to deposit in that investment each month?

N	%i	Pmt	PV	FV
		(?)		
				48.

Answer: Pmt = $184.85.

☛ How long would it take to have $10,000 if you could put $254.22 in the bank each month? (Use the same 6% rate)

N	%i	Pmt	PV	FV
(?)				
				49.

Answer: **N** = 36 months. You see if you have the other figures, you can solve for any of the five parts of a note, just as we solved for **N** in this example.

☛ What interest rate must you earn if you could only put $100 per month in the account but still needed $5000 after 3 years?

N	%i	Pmt	PV	FV
	(?)			
				50.

Answer: **%i** = 21.55%, don't forget to multiply the interest by 12 if your calculator does not do that, and verify that **N** is 36.

☛ Remember that kid you're going to put through college in 12 years from page 53? The current cost of a 4 year college education is still about $45,000. If you have a 6 year old child, and if you predict inflation will be 7% per year, how much will that college education cost when the child is 18 years old. How much must you invest each month at 9% interest to pay for your child's college when she is 18 years old? Does this situation look familiar? We want to go through it again to highlight monthly payments. As in the Present Value example above, this is a two part question.

Part 1: What will the college education cost in 12 years?

What is the future value of $45,000 if you expect inflation and therefore college tuition to go up 7 % per year for the next 12 years until your child is 18?

N	%i	Pmt	PV	FV
12 years	7% inflation	$0	**$45,000**	(?)

Comment: We are looking for the college tuition in 12 years at 7% inflation.

51.

Answer: FV = $101,348 (See page 54.) You must pay $101,348 for your daughter to go to college when she is 18 years old. This is same answer we calculated in the **Present Value** example above.

Part 2: How much do you need to save each month to have $101,348 in 12 years?

Remember, we calculated in the last chapter that you would need $36,032, but like most of us, you don't have that kind of cash at hand. However, you could put a certain amount monthly in an investment that pays 9% annual interest compounded monthly (**%i**). How much must you invest each month (**Pmt**) to have $101,348 (**FV**) in the bank in 12 years (**N**)?

N	%i	Pmt	PV	FV
12 years X 12	9% ÷ 12	(?)	0	101348

Comment: If we need $101,348 in twelve years and can earn 9% annual interest, what payment must we make each month in our 12% investment to have $101,348 in the bank in 12 years?

52.

Answer: Pmt = $393.26 per month. If we put $393.26 every month in an investment that pays 9% annual interest, it will grow to the amount need for tuition, $101,348 in 12 years.

☛ What monthly payment must you put in an investment that pays 20% annual interest to accumulate $1,000,000 in 20 years?

N	%i	Pmt	PV	FV
			(?)	

53.

Answer: Pmt = $321.58 How about that for a retirement plan?

☞ You want to pay all cash for a new Audi Quattro 100LS car for skiing. The car will cost $35,000. You want to buy it in 3 years. You have a discounted note broker "friend" who can invest your monthly payments at 15%. How much should those monthly payments be?

N	%i	Pmt	PV	FV
		(?)		
				54.

Answer: **Pmt** = $775.79

*You can now calculate the amount you need to pay each month in order to have a certain sum in the future. You understand the idea of **Future Value**. That's great! Not only can you use the calculator to figure discount notes, but you can use it for many personal things as well. College education, expensive items such as houses and cars, as well as retirement can all be worked out on your calculator.*

"**When directed and focused, two watts of sun power can burn through steel.**"
Roy Maloney from *Roy's ROT*

Part 2:

Discounting Notes: Or Now We Make Money with Our Calculator

In this section we will begin to use our financial calculator to make intelligent offers on a variety of notes. We will look at discounting cash flows, dealing with uneven cash flows and discounting balloons.

Notes

Chapter 1: Discounting Notes

GOAL: We now present the crux of this book: "How to buy notes at a discount."

• At the end of this lesson, you will understand the basic concept of buying a note at a discount.

• You will understand that you are buying a series of payments, and that series of payments has a Present Value, based on what you want for a yield.

• This lesson will reinforce the concepts of "yield" and "time" when dealing with investments.

TIME: 32 minutes.

Notes

If you were to buy a $20,000 note, 15 year term, 12% interest, monthly payment of $240.03, how would you determine the price? Would you pay $20,000? Or would you pay less? If your investment strategy was to have each invested dollar earn 20%, you couldn't buy that note for "full price," since you would only be getting 12% interest.

To get your 20% return or yield, you would have to pay less than the $20,000. This is the concept of discounting mortgages. Though you pay less for the note, the monthly payments won't change. They'll still be $240.03 each month. So, the question really is: If you're receiving payments of $240.03 for 15 years, how much must you pay to get a 20% yield?

N	%i	Pmt	PV	FV
180	12 ÷ 12	240.03	20000	0

Comment: This is the note you are buying.

55.

We want to calculate the Present Value of this note at our required yield. We put the yield in the **%i** register and then calculate the PV.

N	%i	Pmt	PV	FV
180	1.67	240.03	(?)	0

Comment: However, you must change the **%i** to your yield of 20% divided by 12 and solve for **PV**.

56.

Answer: **PV** = $13,667. By paying $13,667 for this stream of payments you will have a yield of 1.67% per month or 20% per year. This is the offer you would present to the seller of this note.

---Questions and Challenges---

☛ You are offered a $10,000, 12% note, 10 year fully amortizing note with payments of $143.47 per month. You require an 18% yield. What would you pay for this note?

N	%i	Pmt	PV	FV
120	18/12	~143.47	(?)	0
	1.50			

57.

Answer: PV = $7,962.

☛ You are offered a $10,000, 12% note, 10 year fully amortizing note with payments of $143.47 per month. You require an 18% yield. You feel the note is too risky to buy the whole note and decide to only buy part of it. What would you pay for the first 34 payments?

N	%i	Pmt	PV	FV
34	18/12	143.47	(?)	
	1.50			

Comment: Remember **N = 34**, all other amounts remain the same. Now solve for **PV**.

58.

Answer: PV = $3,799 for the first 34 payments.

☞ You receive a phone call from a note holder. She is holding a $36,500 note. The note was created on January 1, 1989. It is now January 1, 1993. The note was written at 12% interest only payments, with the entire principal due seven years from the date of the creation of the note. If you require a 28% yield, what will you pay for this note?

Step # 1: Solve for Payments.

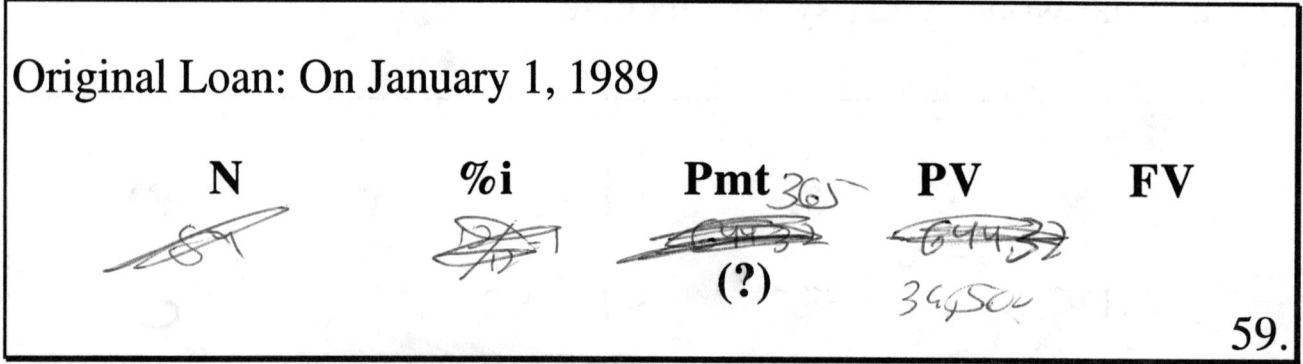

Original Loan: On January 1, 1989

N	%i	Pmt	PV	FV
		(?)		

59.

Answer: Pmt = $365.

Step # 2: Fill in each register as of 1/1/93

Loan *Now:* January 1, 1993: 36 payments remain.

N	%i	Pmt	PV	FV
48	12/12	644.32	24	

Comment: The note was originally written for 84 months on 1/1/89. It is now 1/1/93, 4 years or 48 months later. So 84 months less 48 months means we will collect 36 more payments plus a $36,500 balloon on the 36th payment.

60.

Step # 3: Solve for Present Value (PV)

Your Purchase at a 28% yield:

N	%i	Pmt	PV	FV
= 36	28/12	365	(?)	

Comment: Current **N** = 36

61.

Answer: PV = $24,734.

This situation is very important because you will often get notes that began before NOW and have a due date in the future.

☛ Someone responds to your ad on notes for sale. They need $70,000 to buy a new Mercedes 560SL. They offer you a note with a face value of $97,000. There is no interest to be paid and the entire note will be due on January 1, 1993. It is now July 1, 1991. What interest rate would you earn on this note? This time you must solve for **%i** (first figure what **N** is in months).

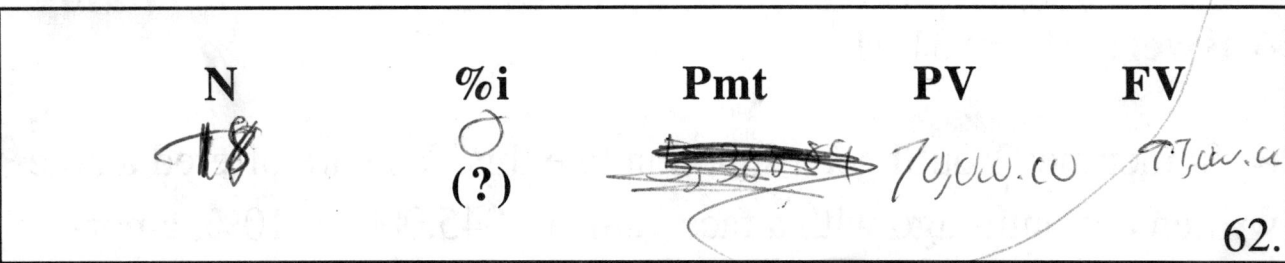

N	%i	Pmt	PV	FV
18	0 (?)	~~5,500.84~~	70,000.00	97,000.00

62.

Answer: **%i** = 21.95%.

☛ You are offered a note written 6 months ago with a face value of
$45,000, at 10%, amortized over 6 years. You require a 22.5% yield
what will you pay for this note?

2PV = I: *= 72*   *PmT = 1,822.34*

Part 1: Original Loan

N	%i	Pmt	PV	FV
72		(?)		

Comment: Remember: 1). You have to figure the **Pmt** first and 2).
that 6 months have gone by.

63.

Answer: **Pmt** is $833.66

Part 2: Present Value (**PV**) after six months.

N	%i	Pmt	PV	FV
66			(?)	

64.

Answer: **PV** = $31,414.

☛ Sometimes You'll get a situation like this: You are offered a note
written 6 months ago with a face value of $45,000, at 10%, amor-

tized over 6 years with payments of $833.66 per month. The seller only wants $15,459 to buy a new Honda. How many payments can you buy, if you require a 22.5% yield?

N	%i	Pmt	PV	FV
(?)	$22.5 \div 12$	833.66	15459	0

65.

Answer: **N** = 23 payments. After 23 payments you return the note to the seller, and she receives the last 43 payments.

☛ Using the above example: What is the balance on the loan after you have received all the payments? (Hint seller received 6 payments and then sold you 23, and then got the note back.)You can get to the answer by figuring **PV** or figuring **FV**. (See page 17 ff.)

N	%i	Pmt	PV	FV
			(?)	

66.

Method #2). (See pages 17 ff.) To figure **PV** you add 23 and 6 and subtract from the original 72 months (6 years) = 43. Then **N** is 43, **%i** is $10 \div 12$, solve for **PV Answer: PV** = 30,024.

N	%i	Pmt	PV	FV
				(?)
				67.

Method #3). (See pages 19 ff.) To solve for **FV**, you add the 6 payments the seller got and the 23 payments you got for a total of 29 which you put under **N**. Put 45,000 under **PV**, and solve for **FV**= $30,024. This will be the balance in 29 months on this loan.

Answer: FV = $30,024.

*You now understand the idea that in buying notes at a discount you are usually buying a series of payment. Sometimes there may be a balloon due as well. What you pay for that series of payments depends on the yield you want on your money. Remember that you can often come upon the same answer through either **PV** or **FV**. This is the start of discounting notes.*

"There are two times in a person's life when he should not speculate: when he can't afford it and when he can."

MARK TWAIN

Notes

Chapter 2: Discounting Balloons

GOAL:

• *At the end of this lesson you will be able to discount a balloon payment to the present.*

• *You will, again, see that money to be received in the future quickly loses its value. The longer you have to wait for your money the less is its Present Value.*

TIME: 13 minutes.

Notes

In purchasing a note you should already be aware that there are several alternative offers you can make on that note. You can purchase only the payments, part of the payments, or only the balloon. In fact, there are many other possibilities we will look at later in the book. However, this is plenty for now. If a note has a balloon payment some time in the future, you can find out the present value of that balloon at your required yield rate.

Example: There is a $50,000 note, interest only at 13%, with a balloon due of $50,000 in 60 months. What would you pay for that balloon if you needed a yield of 18% compounded monthly?

N	%i	Pmt	PV	FV
60 Mnths	18% ÷ 12	0	(?)	$50,000

Comment: We do not care about the monthly payments since we are only buying the balloon. What's the present value of $50,000, 60 months from now at 18% yield?

68.

Answer: PV = $20,465. We will only pay $20,465 for the right to receive $50,000 in 60 months. (This is how savings bonds and zero coupon bonds work. They are purchased at a discount and have a future value.)

Notes

--- Questions and Challenges---

☛ You receive a call from a local Realtor. He tells you he has taken back a $15,000 note for his commission. The terms are: 12.5% interest only for 24 months, with a balloon for the entire amount due at the end of that time period. He would like to continue to receive the payments, but would like to sell you the balloon. If you require a 16% yield, what would you pay for that balloon?

N	%i	Pmt	PV	FV
			(?)	

Comment: The 12.5% (%i) doesn't matter because we aren't dealing with the payments. We only want to buy the balloon.

69.

Answer: PV = $10,915.

☛ What is the balloon payment worth on a 12%, $1,000,000 note with the balloon of $500,000 to be paid in 12 years? You need a yield of 21% compounded monthly?

N	%i	Pmt	PV	FV
			(?)	
				70.

Answer: **PV** = $41,116.

☛ What is $20,000 (**FV**) worth today if you will receive it in 12 months (**N**), and you require a 15% yield (**%i**) compounded monthly?

N	%i	Pmt	PV	FV
			(?)	
				71.

Answer: **PV** = $17,230.

INTERESTING FACT: A note with a balloon payment actually gets more valuable as time passes, because as you get closer to the time the balloon will be paid the note has a greater **Present Value**. So you could buy a balloon, hold it for several months and sell it for more money; even though you sell it at the same yield at which you it. In other words, you would make more money than if you sold it immediately. The opposite is true of an amortizing note. It *decreases* in value as time passes. Can you see why this true?

You now understand that you can buy only the balloon portion of a note. There are times when the seller of a note wants to keep the payments and sell only the balloon. There are times when you would rather not deal with monthly payments but would like a lump sum of money coming to you in the future, especially if you think the note will pay off early. Even though you do not receive the money immediately, you can calculate the value of the balloon today. We did these same exercises when working with Future and Present Values.

> "Money is better than poverty, if only for financial reasons."
> WOODY ALLEN

Notes

Chapter 3: Discounting the Cash Flows

GOAL:

• *At the end of this lesson you will be able to discount the payment stream on a note to its Present Value.*

• *You will understand the value of buying just the payments and leaving a large balloon payment for the seller.*

TIME: 13 minutes.

Notes

As we have seen, you can find the Present Value of a series of payments. This means you can discount the cash flow on a note. As we said earlier, you may sometimes wish to buy just the payments on a note and leave the balloon for the seller.

Example: You are offered a note with a face value of $45,000, paid monthly at 12% interest only, with a balloon payment due 5 years from now. You are willing to buy the payments, but not the balloon. If you require a yield of 19.5% what would you pay for the payments only?

Current loan:

N	%i	Pmt	PV	FV
5 Yrs X 12	12% ÷ 12	(?)	$45,000	$45,000

Comment: We must first find out the amount of the payments we are buying. Remember when any essential component like Payment (**Pmt**) is missing, you must solve for it before proceeding.

72.

Answer: Pmt = $450.

Since we are only buying the payments, we put a 0 under **FV**, 19.5 ÷ 12 under **%i** and solve for Present Value.

N	%i	Pmt	PV	FV
60	1.63	450	(?)	0

73.

Answer: PV = $17,164. We will pay $17,164.80 for the right to receive 60 payments of $450 at 1.63% monthly yield or 19.5% annual yield. At this point you would turn the note back over to the seller who would then receive the balloon.

You can point out to the note seller that he or she is receiving $17,164 cash now, and will get a $45,000 balloon payment in 60 months for a total of $62,164 for a $45,000 note.

--- Questions and Challenges---

☞ If you need an 18% yield, what would you pay for 24 monthly payments of $100?

N	%i	Pmt	PV	FV
			(?)	
				74.

Answer: PV = $2,003.

☞ You are offered a note with the following terms: $169,812.68 face value, amortized over 120 months payable at $2000 per month at 10% annual interest, with a payment of $50,000 due at the end of the 120 months? You need to make 23% on your money? How much will you pay for just the payments with the seller keeping the balloon?

N	%i	Pmt	PV	FV
			(?)	

Comment: Remember to put "0" under **FV** because you are not buying the balloon.

75.

Answer: **PV** = $93,655.

You now understand that when you are presented a note to purchase, you do not have to purchase the whole note (though you may often want to). You can buy a series of payments, e.g., you can buy just the cash flow, just a few payments, just the balloon, or any other combination of terms you are creative enough to think of. All you have to do is discount everything to the Present Value at your desired yield.

"Anyone can make a fortune. It takes a genius to hold on to one."
JAY GOULD

Notes

Chapter 4: Uneven Cash Flows

GOAL:

   • *At the end of this lesson you will understand how to discount more complex notes to find their Present Value.*

   • *You will understand that notes can have several parts, and each part has a Present Value. If you can isolate the parts and then ADD the Present Values, you will know what the whole note is worth to you.*

   • *As in the previous, and next lessons, this lesson will reinforce the concepts of "yield" and "time" when dealing with investments.*

TIME: 31 minutes.

Notes

This chapter of Part 2 may seem a little complicated. However, your trusty financial calculator will not let you down. In fact you may be quite thrilled to see how well it can handle more complex calculations. You may be offered a note that does not have equal regular payments. For example, a note may have interest only payments, and then change to amortizing payments. Or the loan terms may call for large periodic payments. This means the loan does not have level cash flows, and cannot be discounted using the regular keys on the calculator without other steps. Technically, we are discussing the *Internal Rate of Return*. Many calculators have keys that will figure this *IRR* automatically. Here we will use a logical method in which we simply discount the different parts of the note to their present value, at our required yield, and then add the present values.

Example: You are offered a note on developed land in Michigan on a lake. The note is written with a face value of $35,000. The terms are 12.5% interest only for the first 24 months the note then begins amortizing for the next 13 years at 10%. What will you pay for this note if you require a 31% yield? The solution is found in four easy steps:

• **First**, we find the present value of the first part of the note.

• **Second**, we find the present value of the second part of the note which starts in 24 months.

• **Third,** we discount this second part to the present.

• **Fourth**, we add the **Present Values** of the two parts.

This gives us the **Present Value** of the note at our 31% yield.

Step # 1a: Find the Pmt of the First Part

N	%i	Pmt	PV	FV
24	12.5 ÷ 12	(?)	35,000	35,000
				76.

Answer: Pmt = $364.58 The interest only portion of this loan has payments of $364.58. There is no pay-down of principal during the first 24 months, that is why there is a balloon of $35,000.

Step # 1b: Find the PV of the First Part

N	%i	Pmt	PV	FV
24	2.58	**364.58**	(?)	0

Comment: We changed the **%i** to our required yield of 31% divided by 12 months. We put 0 in **FV** because we only want to know what the 24 payments of $364.58 are worth today.

77.

Answer First Part: PV = $6,460.

Step # 2a: Find the Pmt of the Second Part

N	%i	Pmt	PV	FV
13 yrs X 12	10% ÷ 12	(?)	$35,000	0

78.

Answer: Pmt = $401.75. This reflects the second part of the note written at 156 months (13 months X 12), .83% monthly interest. The payments will increase from $364.58 to $401.75 per month.

Step # 2b: Find the PV of the Second Part at Your 31% Yield

N	%i	Pmt	PV	FV
156	2.58	401.75	(?)	0

79.

Answer Second Part: PV = $15,260. At a 2.58% monthly yield or 31% annual yield we will pay $15,260 for the right to receive 156 payments of $401.75. The problem is this part of the note will not begin for 24 months. So, if we will pay $15,260 for the note in 24 months, what will we pay for it now?

Step # 3: Discount the Second Part to the Present

N	%i	Pmt	PV	FV
24	2.58	0	(?)	15260

Comment: We want to know the present value of $15,260 to be received in 24 months at a 31% yield. There are no payments involved since the Present Value takes these into consideration.

80.

Answer: **PV** = $8,274. The present value of the second part of the note is $8,274.22. (Do you understand that the **PV** of the payments is $15,260 from Step #2b above?) However, since that **PV** starts in 24 months we must discount it to the Present.

Step # 4: Adding Present Values

We now add the present value of the first part of the note and the present value of the second part of the note to find the present value of the entire note:

$6,460.94 Present Value of First Part of Note

$8,274.22 Present Value of Second Part of Note.

$14,735.16 Present Value of Entire Note.

We would pay $14,735 for the entire note and would be receiving an annual yield of 31%.

--- Questions and Challenges---

☛ Your Aunt Harriet offers you a new note with a face value of $100,000. For the first five years there are to be interest only payments of $1,000 per month. For the next eight years the note will begin amortizing and will be paid off after the eight years at 10% interest paid monthly. What would you give Aunt Harriet for this note if you require a 21.75% yield? We'll use the same four steps to get the correct amount.

Step # 1: First Five Years

N	%i	Pmt	PV	FV
			(?)	

Comment: Remember you are solving for the **PV** of the first 5 years of payments.

81.

Answer: PV = $36,394.

Step # 2a: Payment on the Amortizing Part

N	%i	Pmt	PV	FV
96		(?)		

Comment: Remember to solve first for **Pmt**.

82.

Answer: Pmt = $1,517.42

Step # 2b: PV of the Amortizing Part

N	%i	Pmt	PV	FV
			(?)	

Comment: Now solve for **PV** at 21.75%.

83.

Answer: PV = $68,794

This is what you would pay to Aunt Harriet if the payments began now. However, the payments won't begin for 60 months on the second part of the loan. So what is the **PV** of $68,794 to be received in 60 months?

Step # 3: PV of the Amortizing Part Now.

N	%i	Pmt	PV	FV
60	21.75 ÷ 12	0	(?)	68794
				84.

Answer: **PV** = $23,414.

Step #4: Add the two present values:

_____

85.

Answer: **PV** = $59,808. This is what you can give to Aunt Harriet and still maintain your 21.75% yield.

☛ You are offered a new note with a face value of $65,384 (**PV**). For the first 36 months (**N**) there are to be interest only payments of $762.81 per month (**Pmt**) at 14% interest. For the next 12 years the note will become amortizing at 11% interest paid monthly with payments of $819.62. What would you pay for this note if you required an 18% yield (**%i**)?

Step # 1: Find the **PV** of the First Part

N	%i	Pmt	PV	FV
	18% ÷ 12		(?)	0

86.

Answer: PV = $21,099.

Step # 2: Find the **PV** of the Second Part.

N	%i	Pmt	PV	FV
			(?)	

87.

Answer: PV = $48,237 in 36 months.

Step # 3: Place answer to Step # 2 in **FV** and discount to the Present by solving for **PV** at the yield of 18% that you require.

N	%i	Pmt	PV	FV
		0	(?)	

88.

Answer: PV = $28,223.

Step # 4: Add the two present values

_____

89.

Answer: PV = $49,322. This is what Aunt Harriet gets and you still get your 18% yield.

You now understand that if you have several different cash flows in a single note, you merely need to separate them, figure their Present Values and add these values together. This will give you the Present Value of the entire note.

I'll bet when you started this chapter, you thought this was going to be too much. When we first got notes like this, we thought we'd never figure them out either. However, now we look forward to "dancing" over the calculator keys and coming up with the correct amount for the yield we want to get. So will you!

"Everything comes to him who hustles while he waits."

THOMAS A. EDISON

Notes

Part 3: Partials

Now The Fun Really Begins and The Imagination Soars

It is possible to buy just parts of a note. You are only limited by your imagination and your ability to calculate the **Present Value** in making offers to buy "partials." For example, you can buy:

- The first half of the payment stream
- You can buy the last half of the payment stream,
- You can buy one half of the first one half of the payments,
- You can buy just the balloon,
- Just the payments,
- Half of the balloon, etc.

Notes

Chapter 1: Buying Partials

GOAL:

• *At the end of this lesson you will understand how to calculate the Present Value of any part of a note.*

• *You will, again, see that by buying only part of a note and leaving the residual, or "back end" for the note seller you will be able to buy notes with a very small perceived discount.*

TIME: 39 minutes.

Notes

The most valuable and powerful part of this book is understanding how to buy parts of a note. By buying *partials* you are able to maintain high yields on your purchases, yet turn the note back to the note seller with a high balance due. The seller may perceive that they are not even taking a discount. If people advertise that they will buy a note with "no discount" they are probably offering to buy a partial. This is a dishonest form of advertising, because the note seller is indeed taking a discount. But that discount is apparent only to the sophisticated note investor.

For the next several chapters we will work with this extended example of buying a partial note.

You have an opportunity to buy a well secured $15,000, 13%, 30 year mortgage. You need a 25% yield.

Original Loan

N	%i	Pmt	PV	FV
30 years X 12	13% ÷ 12 mnth	(?)	15000	0

Comment: First we must find the monthly payment on this loan. This is a fully amortizing loan, so there is no **FV** or balloon payment.

90.

Answer: Pmt = $165.93.

We want to buy this note to yield us 25%.

N	%i	Pmt	PV	FV
360	25% ÷ 12	**165.93**	(?)	0

Comment: We are looking for the amount we will pay for this income stream at a 25% yield.

91.

Answer: PV = $7,959. This $15,000 loan is only worth $7,959 to us if we want a 25% yield. The reason it is worth so little is that it is a very long term, 30 year loan. This is the *time value of money* telling us that money that is to be received 30 years from now is not worth much now.

The problem is:
- your note seller may not want to sell the note to you at such a deep discount,
- you do not want to invest for such a long period time, and
- You may not want to invest that much money.

The answer to this and similar problems is to buy a **partial**. What would happen if we bought only the next 5 years worth of payments?

N	%i	Pmt	PV	FV
5 yrs X 12	25% ÷ 12	165.93	(?)	0

Comment: How much will we pay for the next 60 payments of $165.93 so that we will still get a yield of 25%.

92.

Answer: PV = $5,653. This means we would pay $5,653 for the next 5 years of payments, and the note holder gets to keep the remaining payments.

--- Questions and Challenges---

We are still working with this note:

PV = $15,000, **%i** =13%, **N** = 30 year mortgage, **Pmt** = $165.93.
You need a 25% yield. Remember, we paid $5,653 for the next 60
payments.

☞ What is the balance on the above note when we turn it back to the
seller after 60 months?

N	%i	Pmt	PV	FV
360 minus 60 mnths	13% ÷ 12	165.93	(?)	0
				93.

Answer: PV = $14,712. Because we have changed **N** to 300 and
calculated **PV** we know that the remaining balance on this note when
we turn it back to the seller will be $14,712. As you can see, the
payor has paid down very little principal. You can now show the
seller of this $15,000 note that she will receive $5,653 in cash from
you now and a loan with an outstanding balance of $14,712 after five
years. She is hardly taking a discount from her standpoint.

Summary:

You get 60 payments of $165.93 for a 25% yield.

Cost to you: $5,653 for a 25% yield.

Seller gets: $5,653 Cash Now

$14,714 loan back in 60 months

(original balance was $15,000)

$20,367 TOTAL CASH TO SELLER

FOR A $15,000 NOTE!!!

You can see that from the point of view of the seller, this offer is much more attractive than the $7,959 we calculated first for the whole note. Therefore, you will often find partial purchases more acceptable to the note seller.

> "I hate this damn computer,
> I wish that they would sell it.
> It never does what I want it to
> Only what I tell it!"

Notes

Chapter 2:

Buying the last half of the payment stream

GOAL:

    • *At the end of this session you will understand how to calculate the last part of a payment stream and then discount that figure back to the present.*

    • *You will be able to find the Present Value of payments that start sometime in the future and then discount that figure to NOW.*

TIME: 18 minutes.

Notes

You can buy any part of the payment stream, simply by discounting it to the present. Here is the **Sample Note**.

N	%i	Pmt	PV	FV
360	13% ÷ 12	165.93	15000	0

94.

If the seller of the above note (the same one we used in Chapter 1) wants cash now in a lump sum, but also wants to receive payments from the note, what can we do? We could offer to buy the *last* 180 payments and give him cash now. This is a two step process: we need to find the Present Value of the income stream, and then the Present Value of that *Present Value* since it won't start for 180 months. We think you will find the final answer very interesting. We still want a 25% yield.

Part 1: PV of 180 payments:

N	%i	Pmt	PV	FV
180 months	25% ÷ 12	165.93	(?)	0

Comment: We know we will buy 180 payments of $165.93 at a 25% yield. The **PV** will tell what that is worth for 180 months of payments.

95.

Answer: PV = $7,769. If we pay $7,769 for 180 payments of $165.93, we will be making 25% on our money. However, this payment stream does not start for 180 months, so we must discount this figure to the present.

Part 2: Discount to the Present:

N	%i	Pmt	PV	FV
180	2.08	0	(?)	7769

Comment: The note is worth $7,769 in 180 months, to find out what $7,769 is worth today we move that figure to **FV** and calculate **PV**. **Pmt** becomes 0 because we are only trying to find out what $7,769 is worth today.

96.

Answer: PV = $189.91. Do you think your note seller would sell the last 180 payments for $189? Probably not. The point is, you will seldom be able to buy the *back half* of a 20 year long note. The discount would simply be too great.

The important point is to see the power of the *time-value-of-money*. $7,769 to be received in 180 months is almost worthless today. It is only worth $189.

--- Questions and Challenges---

☛ Aunt Harriet has an $11,000 note written at 13.5% annual interest. It is payable monthly and is fully amortized over 36 months. She wants to sell you the last 18 payments. You need a 28% yield. What will you pay for these 18 payments?

Step # 1: Find the **Pmt** on the current note:

N	%i	Pmt	PV	FV
		(?)		
				97.

Answer: Pmt = $373.29

Step # 2: Find the **PV** on 18 payments at 28% yield:

N	%i	Pmt	PV	FV
			(?)	
				98.

Answer: **PV** = $5,435.75

Step # 3: Discount to today:

N	%i	Pmt	PV	FV
			(?)	

Comment: Since the payments don't start for 18 months, we must discount them to today.

99.

Answer: PV = $3,588

Step # 4: What is the balance on the loan when you get the note from the seller in 18 months?

N	%i	Pmt	PV	FV
			(?)	

100.

Answer: PV = $6,051

Summary:

You get 18 payments of $373 starting in 18
months for a cost of $3,588 *now* at a yield of
28%.

Seller, Aunt Harriet, gets the $3,588 now and 18
payments of $373. After she has received the
18 payments, she will turn the note over to you.

*No matter where the calculations take you, it always ends up in the same place. What is the **Present Value**? In other words, how much will you give the seller **NOW** to get the yield you desire?*

"Progress always involves risk. You can't steal second base and keep your foot on first."
---FREDERICK WILCOX

Notes

Chapter 3: Buying Part of the Payment

GOAL:

   • *At the end of this session you will see that you can buy part of the regular payments and let the seller keep the other part.*

TIME: 12 minutes.

Notes

You can buy part of the payment on a note, and let the seller have the other part. In this way the seller can get cash now, and still retain some income from the note.

You are offered a $100,000 first note, amortized over 30 years at 10% with monthly payments of $877.57 per month. The seller needs $300 per month to make his car payment and $5,000 cash down for the car, (remember that Mercedes 560 SLE). You are willing to invest your money at 19%.

N	%i	Pmt	PV	FV
360	.83	877.57	**100000**	0

Comment: This is the original note.

101.

You will buy the entire note, but give the seller what he wants from the note and you keep what is left. We will calculate your yield based on what you get from the payor minus what you give the note seller. In this case you give the seller $5,000 cash. You receive $877 each month from the Payor. You give $300 to the seller leaving you with $577 per month.

Payor pays $877 per month
Seller gets $300 per month
You get $577 per month

☛If you require a 19% yield how many payments should you buy?

N	%i	Pmt	PV	FV
(?)	1.58	($877.57 - $300)	5000	0

Comment: By solving for **N**, the number of payments you are buying, you can buy just part of the note, and just part of the payments.

102.

Answer: **N** = 9.38. If you buy 9.38 months of the payments of $577.57 for $5,000, you will have a yield of 1.58% per month or 19% per year. What should you do about the .38 fraction of the month? Because you can't collect a .38 part of a month, you round it up in your favor to 10 months of payments and this greatly increases your yield. Put 10 in **N** and solve for **%i**.

N	%i	Pmt	PV	FV
10	2.71	577.57	**5000**	0

103.

Comment: You are now making 2.71% yield or 32.54% annual yield by buying 10 payments of $577.57. The seller of the note gets his $5,000 and $300 per month. You turn the note back to him after you have received the 10 payments. You get a 32+% yield.

103.

Summary:

You get: 10 payments of $577.57 for a 32% yield. Cost to you: $5,000.

Seller gets: $5,000 Cash Now

10 payments of $300 each

350 payments of $877.57

EXAMPLE: You get a call from Aunt Harriet. She has a $50,000 note written at 12% interest only with payments of $500 per month, and the balance of $50,000 due 60 months from now. She is willing to sell ½ of the payment or $250 per month, but doesn't want to sell the balloon. You need a 32% yield. What can you give her for these payments?

You must figure the **PV**, since you know the payments are ½ of $500 for 60 months, your yield is 32% ÷ 12 or 2.67% per month.

N	%i	Pmt	PV	FV
60	2.67%	$250	(?)	0

104.

Answer: PV = $7,442.13

Summary:

You get: 60 payments of $250 for a 32% yield.
Cost to you: $7,442.13

Seller , Aunt Harriet, gets: $7,442.13 cash now
60 payments of $250 each month
$50,000 balloon payment

This offer should look very attractive to her.

--- Questions and Challenges---

☞ A note seller has a note that pays $1,000 per month. He wants to sell you 50 payments of $500. You need a yield of 25%. What will you pay him?

N	%i	Pmt	PV	FV
			(?)	
				105.

Answer: **PV** = $15,440.

Using the above note, suppose the seller needs $10,000. How many payments will you buy if you want a 20% yield?

N	%i	Pmt	PV	FV
(?)				
				106.

Answer: N = 11. Then you will return the note to the seller.

You now understand that you can buy part of the payment on the note and let the note seller receive part of the payment. You can still get the yield you want, and the note seller can get the cash he or she wants.

From your point of view, the common denominator remains the "yield," the percentage you want to make on the note. Mathematically, the calculations result in the same yield whether you are making a partial purchase or a whole purchase.

"Saving is a very fine thing. Especially when your parents have done it for you."
WINSTON CHURCHILL

Chapter 4: Buying Part of the Balloon

Now let's put together our study of Present Value and Future Value

GOAL:

*• At the end of this session you will be able to calculate what **Part** of a balloon is worth today.*

• You will be able to make an offer on a note where you get part of the balloon and the seller gets the rest of the balloon.

TIME: 14 minutes.

Notes

Just as in buying part of the regular payments, you can buy part of the balloon payment. If the seller needs some cash now, but is unable to give up the income from the note, you can give him some cash now for a part (or all) of the balloon when it's paid. The problem with buying all or part of a balloon is, as we have seen, it is not worth very much. Because of the *time-value-of money*, money to be received in the future discounts very quickly and the seller may not want to take a large perceived discount. Nonetheless, this may be a viable strategy in some instances.

Example: You are offered a note by your Aunt Harriet with the following terms: $50,000 face value, interest only at 12% paid at $500 per month with a balloon due of $50,000 in 36 months. What would you give her for $25,000 of the balloon if you required a 24% yield?

You are looking for the **PV** of a $25,000 balloon (**FV**) to be received in 36 months at 2% yield per month.

N	%i	Pmt	PV	FV
36	2	0	(?)	25000

Comment: There are no payments; they are all going to the note seller. **FV** is $25,000 or ½ of the balloon; the other half goes to the Seller.

107.

Answer: PV = $12,255. You will pay $12,255 for the right to receive $25,000 in 36 months. This gives you a 24% yield.

Summary:

You get: $25,000 in 36 months for a 24% yield.
Cost to you: $12,255.

Seller, Aunt Harriet, gets: $12,255 cash now
36 payments of $500
$25,000 balloon payment in 36 months
(½ of the $50,000 balloon).

What if Aunt Harriet had wanted $18,000? How much of the balloon would you have taken?

In this case you know the **PV** ($18,000, that's what you must give Aunt Harriet) and you want to know the **FV**.

N	%i	Pmt	PV	FV
36	2	0	18000	(?)

108.

Answer: **FV** = $36,717. You will receive $36,717 in 36 months, and the note seller will receive the rest or $13,282 ($50,000 minus $36,717).

Summary:

You get: $36,717 in 36 months for a 24% yield.
Cost to you: $18,000.

Seller, Aunt Harriet, gets: $18,000 cash now, then
36 payments of $500 and a
$13,282 balloon payment in 36 months

--- Questions and Challenges---

☛ A note seller has a note with a $100,000 balloon payment in 60 months. How much will you give him for $75,000 of that if you need a 18% yield?

N	%i	Pmt	PV	FV
			(?)	
				109.

Answer: PV = $30,697

☛ A young man has a guaranteed inheritance of $1,000,000 from his Aunt Harriet in 30 years. What will you give him for $500,000 of that inheritance if you require a 19% yield compounded monthly?

N	%i	Pmt	PV	FV
			(?)	
				110.

Answer: **PV** = $1,749. ($500,000 to be received in 30 years is only worth $1,749 today.) Hardly worth it, is it?

You now understand that you can buy just about any part of a note that meets the seller's needs and your yield requirements. You also understand that balloons to be received far in the future are not worth very much today, i.e., their Present Value is low.

> Money is like manure. If you spread it around it does a lot of good, but if you pile it up in one place it stinks like hell.
> —Clint Murchinson

Notes

Chapter 5: Split Funding

GOAL:

> • *At the end of this lesson you will understand how to buy part of a note now and part in the future and still maintain a high yield.*

> • *You will see how it is possible to buy a note and yet give the seller "full face value" for that note.*

TIME: 29 minutes.

Notes

SEE **APPENDIX #3** FOR ANSWERS TO ALL **QUESTIONS AND CHALLENGES** BY BOX NUMBER.

The more flexible you are in your ability to make a variety of offers, the better your chances are of getting one of your offers accepted by the seller. Giving two or three options move the seller away from a "yes" or "no" to a choice of "either/or". This gives you the best chance of fulfilling the needs of the seller and buying the note.

You are offered a note with a face value of $100,000 amortized over 30 years, at 10%, payments are $877.57 per month. You need a 26% yield. What would you pay for the whole note?

N	%i	Pmt	PV	FV
360	.83	877.57	100000	0

Comment: This is the original note.

111.

You must change the yield to 26% per year or 2.17% per month

N	%i	Pmt	PV	FV
360	2.17	877.57	(?)	0

112.

Answer: PV = $40,485.   You can pay $40,485 for this loan.

The seller perceives this as a 60% discount on the $100,000 note. He often cannot grasp the *time value of money* and how the 30 years before he receives his full payment seriously erodes this note. Therefore, he may not be willing to give you such a big discount. So you can offer to buy ½ of the note *now* and ½ in 180 months.

You keep your same yield but change the **N** to ½ of the original **N** and solve for what you would pay for this note.

N	%i	Pmt	PV	FV
180	2.17	877.57	39648	0

Comment: You would pay $39,648 for the first ½ of this note or 180 payments, and then return the note to the seller.

113.

The seller is amazed. He gets $39,640 NOW and there will still be a balance of $81,665 on the second 180 payments. We'll leave it to you to verify the balance of this note after 180 payments have been received.

Another variation is to offer to buy ⅓ of the note now, ⅓ when you have received ⅓ of the payments, ⅓ when you have received ⅔ of the payments.

You keep your same yield but change the **N** to ⅓ of the original **N** (360 ÷ 3 = 120) and solve for what you would pay for this *part* note.

N	%i	Pmt	PV	FV
120	2.17	877.57	(?)	0

114.

Answer: PV = $37,410. You would pay **$37,410** for the first ⅓ of this note. When you have received the *first* third, you would buy the *second* third for the same price and then the *last* third for the same price.

The seller erroneously adds up the three payments he will receive and thinks he is getting more than the face value of the note. In fact, he is getting the same price with each of these options, and you continue to get a 26% yield.

SUMMARY: In split funding this note three times:

> *You* get: 120 payments of $877.57 for a 26% yield. Cost to you: $37,410 AND you have the right to make the same purchase two more times in 120 more months and 240 months.

> *Seller* gets: $37,410 Now
> $37,410 in 120 months
> <u>$37,410 in 240 months</u>
> $112,230 *Total Cash To Seller For The $100,000 Note!*

--- Questions and Challenges---

☞ A note seller has a note with payments of $568.30 per month, at 11% interest amortized over 180 months. The face value of the note is $50,000. You need a yield of 27%. What would you pay for the *entire* note?

N	%i	Pmt	PV	FV
			(?)	
				115.

Answer: **PV** = $24,797. The seller sees that this is over a 50% discount.

☞ Well, that's one option, but let's explore split funding again. The seller thinks this is too large a discount. You offer to buy ½ the note now and ½ when you had received ½ of the payments. What will you pay for ½ of the note?

N	%i	Pmt	PV	FV
			(?)	
				116.

Answer: PV = $21,848

☛ The note seller still balks. You offer to buy ¼ of the payments now and ¼ after each ¼ of the payments had been made. What will you offer for ¼ of the note?

N	%i	Pmt	PV	FV
			(?)	
				117.

Answer: PV = $15,977 for the $50,000 note. In this example you can tell the seller, "I will give you $63,911.29 ($15,977.78 x 4) if you are willing to be flexible about when you receive the payments." The seller sees $63,911.29 and the original amount was only $50,000 and she will often accept this offer!

☛ To show how profitable split funding is supposing you were to split fund the note every month. Put 1 in **N**, 2.25 in **%i**, $568.30 remains in **Pmt** and solve for **PV**.

N	%i	Pmt	PV	FV
			(?)	
				118.

Answer: **PV** = \$555. You receive a payment of \$568.30 from the payor each month and only pay out \$555.70 to the seller of the note. You are really using the seller of the note's money to pay her. This is, of course, not possible. No note seller would do this; but it does show why you can *split fund* at such a profit.

INTERESTING FACT: If you buy one half of the payments on a note for one half of the balance due, your yield will be double the interest rate on the note. For example, if you are offered a \$10,000 note, written at 10% interest, amortized over 20 years, and you bought 10 years worth of monthly payments for \$5,000 your yield would be 20% per year. If you bought ⅓ of the payments for ⅓ of the balance your yield would be 30%. If you bought ¼ of the payments for ¼ of the balance your yield would be 40%. We hope you know enough now to verify that for yourself on your calculator.

You now understand that paying for part of the note now and part later allows the note seller to perceive that he or she is not even taking a discount on the note. You now understand the "time value of money" at a more profound level.

Notes

Part 4:

Loan to Value

GOAL: Safety and Notes

• *At the end of this section you will understand the most important concept related to the safety of your investments, viz. the amount of equity protecting your note.*

• *You will be able to explain the difference between Loan to Value and Investment to Value.*

• *You will be introduced to the idea of using investors to buy your notes. You will see how you can earn a cash flow and spend none of your own money.*

TIME: 31 minutes.

Notes

SEE **APPENDIX #3** FOR ANSWERS TO ALL **QUESTIONS** AND **CHALLENGES** BY BOX NUMBER.

Chapter 1

Loan to Value

A very important concept in the discounted note business is the *loan-to-value ratio* of the note you are buying. This is the total of your loan, and all *senior loans** divided by the fair market value of the property. The lower the *loan-to-value ratio* is the safer your loan, the more equity there is in the property and the less likely you are to lose money if there is a foreclosure.

☛ You are offered a $50,000 second note, behind a $100,000 first note. You know the property is valued at $300,000. What is the loan to value ratio?

Answer: $150,000 in loans divided by $300,000 value of the property equals .50 or 50% L-T-V.

☛ You are offered a Second note for $15,000 on a home valued at $75,000. There is a first loan of $50,000. What is the *loan-to-value ratio?*

| first loan | + | second loan = | total of all loans | ÷ | prop value | = L-T-V |

Answer: 87%

119.

Senior loans are those loans that were placed on the property before yours. Thus a 1st mortgage is senior to a 2nd mortgage and a 2nd mortgage is junior to a 1st mortgage.

☛ You are offered a second note for $25,000 on a home valued at $200,000 There is a first of $50,000, your note, and a third for $75,000. What is the loan to value?

---

first loan   +   second loan =   total of all loans   ÷   prop value   = L-T-V

120.

Answer: 38%. The third loan is not part of your calculations. You only use the loans *senior* to your loan.

Chapter 2

Loan-to-Value Guide Lines

We have not said much about investors until now so we could focus on the calculator. However, most of us will be **brokering** notes to private or commercial investors. We need to be aware of their guidelines and how much they will invest in a note. Most investors have L-T-V guidelines. For example, an investor might not invest if the loan to value ratio is higher than 75% on a single family home, or 65% on a small apartment building, or 50% on land. It is important to understand these guidelines when making a bid on a note.

A more accurate term might be *investment-to-value ratio*, rather than *loan-to-value ratio*. If you had a $50,000 note but were only paying $35,000 for it, that would be the figure you would use in your calculations.

☛ You are offered a second note for $50,000 on a home valued at $150,000. There is a first note of $75,000. You will pay $35,000 for the second note. What is your *investment to value*?

first loan   + cost of 2nd loan =   total of all loans   ÷   prop value   = I-T-V

Answer: 73%. To find the I-T-V (not the L-T-V) you divide the amount you are paying plus all senior loans divided by the price of the property.   121.

☛ What is the *investment-to-value* of your purchase of a second note with a face value of $100,000, that you pay $64,325.21 for, if the first is for $123,456 and home has a "quick sale"* appraisal for $321,000?

first loan   + cost of 2nd loan = total of all loans   ÷   prop value   = I-T-V

Answer: 58%.   122.

Quick sale is the price you could get for property in the event it was necessary to quickly sell that property rather than waiting for the best offer.

Chapter 3

Calculating How Much to Invest

Sooner or later (sooner for most) you will run out of your own money. In fact, most people in the note business use institutional and/or private investors. Investors usually like a yield of 13% to 17%. It is now possible to put together everything you have learned so that you can make reasonable offers on notes. These offers must allow you to resell or broker the notes at a profit. To do this you must know the L-T-V ratios required by the investors in your notes and not exceed that L-T-V when you buy the note. There are *five* steps to buying notes that you can resell.

1). Figure the parameters of the note you wish to buy: (**N, %i, PV, Pmt, FV**)

2). Figure the current L-T-V on the property. Is it low enough to allow you to buy the note?

3). Figure the *Investor's* L-T-V on the property minus any loans that are senior to the loan you are considering. This is the maximum you can invest in this note and still resell it at a profit to an investor.

4). Using this maximum L-T-V figure, calculate how much of the note you can buy using your investor's yield.

5). Subtract your profit from this figure, and offer this to the note seller.

EXAMPLE 1: You have an investor who will buy your notes from you at a 14% yield. He will only buy if the property has a loan to value ratio of 75% on single family homes that are owner occupied.

A free and clear house sold one year ago in San Francisco, CA for $345,000. The sellers accepted $25,000 cash down. The buyers took over a $250,000 first loan and the sellers carried back a second note for the balance at 10% interest only, payable monthly, with a balloon due 5 years from close of escrow. You have no cash but would like to resell the note to your investor. What is your offer?

Step # 1: Figure the parameters of the second note.

The amount of the note is *purchase price* less *down payment* and *other loans*. $345,000 - $25,000 cash *down* less the *first loan* of $250,000 equals a $70,000 second note.

Step # 2: What is the current L-T-V on this property?

$250,000	+	$70,0000	=	$320,000	÷	$345,000	=	**93%**
first loan	+ cost of 2nd loan	=	total of all loans ÷	prop value	=	L-T-V

This property already has a "loan to value" ratio of 93% and that is too high for your investor. You cannot buy this note.

EXAMPLE 2: Same as above, but the house is now worth more money. You have an investor who will buy your notes from you at a 14% yield but must have a loan to value ratio of 75% on single family homes that are owner occupied.

A free and clear house sold one year ago in San Francisco, CA for $420,000. The sellers accepted $100,000 cash down. The buyers took over a $250,000 first loan and the sellers carried back a second note for the balance at 10% interest only, payable monthly, with a balloon due 5 years from close of escrow. You have no cash but would like to resell the note to your investor. What is your offer to the note seller?

Step # 1: Figure the parameters of the second note.

The amount of the note is: *purchase price* less *down payment and other loans*. $420,000 - $100,000 cash down less the *first loan* of $250,000 equals $70,000 for the second note.

N	%i	Pmt	PV	FV
60	.83	(?)	70,000	70,000

123.

Answer: Pmt = $583.33. Payments on the current note are $583.33 per month

Step # 2: What is the current L-T-V on this property?

$250,000	+	$70,0000	=	$320,000	÷	$420,000	=	**76%**
first loan	+	cost of 2nd loan	= total of all loans	÷		prop value	=	L-T-V

The L-T-V is still above 75%. However, you will remember above that what is important is the I-T-V (*Investment to Value*). Let's continue our calculations and see what is possible.

Step # 3: Calculate 75% of the price of the property and subtract all the loans senior to the one you wish to buy. That is the amount you can invest.

$420,000	X	.75	-	$250,000	=	$65,000
Prop. Price	X	L-T-V	-	senior loans	=	Maximum you can invest.

The maximum amount the investor will pay is $65,000. What is the interest rate your investor needs? 14 per cent. We must now calculate how much of the note the investor can buy for $65,000. Can he buy the entire note?

Step # 4: What is the present value of this note at 14%? (Remember 1 year has gone by, so **N** is now 60 - 12 = 48 months.)

N	%i	Pmt	PV	FV
48	1.17	583.33	(?)	70000

124.

Answer: **PV** = $61,461. Therefore, this note is within the parameters of your investor, and it would be possible to purchase the entire note. This is an important lesson in the difference between *Loan to Value* and *Investment to Value*.

Step # 5: What is your profit?

You require a 7% commission on the $61,461.

$61,461 times 7% equals $4,302

You offer the note seller $61,461 less $4,302 or $57,159 net to the seller. The *Investor* gives you $61,461, and you give the *Seller* $57,159 and keep the $4,302 difference as your *commission*.

Summary:

You get: a $4,302 Commission.

Seller gets: $57,159 Cash Now

Investor gets: 48 payments of $583.33 and a
balloon of $70,000 for a cost of $61,461 at a
14% annual yield.

---Questions and Challenges---

☛ Mr. and Mrs. Flintstone sold their New Jersey home to Mr. Rubble for $250,000. They accepted $80,000 cash down and carried a note for the balance at 10% interest and amortized over 20 years. One day after the sale closes the Flintstones have a sudden emergency and need cash quickly. They must now sell their note immediately. What will you offer them? You will get a 7% commission. Your investor will not go past 55% loan to value and needs a 14% yield.

Step # 1: Calculate the parameters of the note.

The amount of the note is Purchase Price less Down Payment and other loans.

N	%i	Pmt	PV	FV
		(?)		170000

Comment: What is the **Pmt**?

125.

Answer: Pmt = $1,640.54

Step # 2: What is the current L-T-V on this property?

170,000	+	0	=	170,000	÷	250,000	=	68%
first loan	+	cost of 2nd loan	= total of all loans	÷	prop value	=	L-T-V

Step # 3: Calculate 55% (Your investor's required L-T-V) of the price of the property and subtract all the loans senior to the one you wish to buy. That is the amount you can invest.

250,000	X	.55	-	0	=	137,500
Prop. Price	X	L-T-V	- senior loans	=	Maximum you or your investor can invest.

The maximum amount the investor will pay is: $_____.

Step # 4: How many payments can you buy?

You will calculate the **PV** of the payments only, at a 14% yield

N	%i	Pmt	PV	FV
240	1.17	1640.54	(?)	0

126.

Answer: PV = $131,926. Which is less than the 55% L-T-V. This is what the investor will pay for 240 payments of $1,640.54 to receive his 14% yield.

Step # 5: What is your commission: We require a 7% commission of:

_____ times 7% equals *$9,234.87.*

We offer the note seller $_____ less $_____ commission or $_____ net to the seller.

Answer: Net to the seller = $122,691.

Commission to you = $9,234.87

You now should see the power of using investors to invest in the notes you buy. By earning commissions you do not need to use any of your own money.

"To be successful you have to be lucky, or a little mad, or very talented or find yourself in a rapid-growth field."

EDWARD De BONO

Notes

Part 5:

Notes in the REAL World

GOAL: The Final Part

   • *At the end of this Part, you will be able to calculate several purchase offers on real notes.*

   • *You will see the value of making two or three offers on the same note to meet the needs of the seller, yet keep your high yields.*

   • *You will understand that you can broker a note and never own it. Or you can buy a note at one price and resell it to an investor for a higher price.*

   • *You will be a professional note buyer, able to reduce any income stream to its Present Value.*

TIME: 2 notes: 25 minutes each.

Notes

Note 1:

Calculating offers on a fully amortizing note.

You are approached by a real estate broker who has a note for sale on a single family home in North Carolina. The home just sold for $250,000 with the buyer getting a new bank loan for $172,500, and the seller is carrying back a new second loan for $15,000 at 11% amortized over 15 years with monthly payments of $170.49 per month. You have an investor who will only invest in notes where there is at least a 75% loan to value ratio and he wants to make 17% on his investment. If you need a 27% yield, think of four offers you could make on this note, to allow you to resell to the investor.

Offer 1:

Offer to buy the whole note

Step # 1: What is the Loan to Value ratio on the property now?

Step # 2: What could you offer for the whole note?

Step # 3: What would your investor pay for the whole note?

Step # 4: What is your dollar profit if you sold the entire note to the investor?

ANSWER: (Buying the whole note)

Step # 1:

Total of all loans: ($172,500 + $15,000) = 187,500 ÷ $250,000 purchase price = **75% loan to value**. So both you and your investor would be comfortable buying the entire note.

Step # 2:

N	%i	Pmt	PV	FV
15 years X 12	11% ÷ 12	170.49	15000	0

Comment: This is the current loan. We must substitute our required yield in the **%i** register on the calculator.

127.

You want a 27% yield (2.25% per month.)

N	%i	Pmt	PV	FV
180	2.25	170.49	(?)	0

128.

Answer: PV = $7,439. You can pay $7,439 for this note. You will then have the right to receive 180 payments of $170.49, giving you a yield of 2.25% per month or 27% per year. If our investor will buy this same note at a 17% yield how much will he pay?

Step # 3:

N	%i	Pmt	PV	FV
180	17% ÷ 12	170.49	(?)	0

Comment: You simply change our 27% yield to the investor's 17% yield and solve for **PV** to see what he will pay.

129.

Answer: PV = $11,077. The investor can pay $11,077 for this note. He will then have the right to receive 180 payments of $170.49, giving him a yield of 1.425 per month or 17% per year. What is your dollar profit?

Step # 4:

If the investor will pay $11,077 for this note, and you bought it for $7,439.24, you will make a profit of **$3,638.67** on the sale to your 17% investor.

Summary:

You get: profit of $3,638.67

Seller gets: $7,439.24 *cash NOW*

Investor gets: 180 payments of $170.49 for a
17% yield. Cost to investor: $11,077.91

The owner/seller of this note may not be willing to sell a $15,000 note for $7,439. He or she may think this discount is too large. So you can make an offer to buy only part of the note.

Offer 2:

Offer to buy one half of the payments

This is the original note.

N	%i	Pmt	PV	FV
180	.92	170.49	**15000**	0

130.

To buy half the payments at a 27% yield, you must change the **N** to 90 and the **%i** to 27% and solve for **PV**.

N	%i	Pmt	PV	FV
90	2.25	170.49	(?)	0

131.

Answer: PV = $6,554. This means you will pay $6,554 for the right to receive the next 90 payments of $170.49 at a 27% annual yield.

After you have received the 90 payments, you would turn the note back to the seller. What would be the balance owed then?

N	%i	Pmt	PV	FV
90	11%	170.49	(?)	0

Comment: If there are 90 payments remaining, by solving for **PV**, you will know the remaining balance on the note to be turned back to the seller.

132.

Answer: PV = $10,417. The seller now has the note back and the right to collect the remaining 90 payments of $179.49 at a .92% monthly yield or 11% annual yield. You can explain to the seller that he received $6,904.11 from you and will receive a note with a balance of $10,417.50 in 90 months so he is "really" not taking a discount at all.

Offer 3:

Offer to Buy the Note and Then Resell to an Investor

"Buy-Sell" Profits: What if you sold the 90 payments to your 17% investor?

N	%i	Pmt	PV	FV
90	1.42	170.49	(?)	0
				133.

Answer: PV = $8,641. The investor is willing to pay $8,641.53 for the right to receive the 90 payments at a monthly yield of 1.42% or 17% annually.

Since you bought the 90 payments at a 27% yield or $6,904.11, and are selling them at a 17% yield or $8,641.53 your buy/sell profit is: $1,737.42.

Summary:

Yo u get: a profit of $1,737.42

Seller gets: $6,904.11 Cash Now

$10,417.50 loan balance in 90 months

Investor gets: 90 payments of $170.49 for a 17%

yield at a cost of: $8,641.53

Offer 4:

Offer to buy ½ of each monthly payment, with other half remaining with the seller

N	%i	Pmt	PV	FV
180	.92	170.49	15000	0

Comment: This is the original note. To buy half the monthly payments at a 27% yield we must change the **Pmt** to half of $170.49 or $85.25 and the **%i** to 27% and solve for **PV**.

134.

N	%i	Pmt	PV	FV
180	2.25	85.25	(?)	0

135.

Answer: PV = $3,719. For $3,719 you will have the right to receive the next 180 payments of $85.25. If the seller does not like this, you can buy one half of just the first 90 payments. It would look like this:

N	%i	Pmt	PV	FV
90	2.25	85.25	(?)	0

136.

Answer: PV = $3,277. This should look attractive to the seller. He will get $3,277 in cash from us now. He will get the other half of the payment of $85.25 each month, and after you have received the 90 payments, he would get the note back with a balance due of $10,417.50.

BUY/SELL PROFIT: What if you sold the 90 payments to your 17% investor?

You change the **%i** to the investors yield of 17% and solve for **PV** to see what he would pay:

N	%i	Pmt	PV	FV
90	1.42	85.25	(?)	0

137.

Answer: PV = $4,321. Your investor will pay $4,321.02 for the right to receive 90 payments of $85.25.

Since you bought the 90 payments at a 27% yield or $3,277.23, and are selling them at a 17% yield or $4,321.02, your buy/sell profit is: $1,044.

Summary:

You get: buy/sell profit of $1,044

Seller gets: $3,277.23 Cash Now
$85.25 per month for the next 90 months
$10,417.50 loan balance in 90
months

Investor gets: 90 payments of $85.25 for a 17%
yield at a cost of: $4,321.02

Offer 5:

Split Funding

You can also offer to give the seller of the note some cash now and some cash in the future. This split funding technique is very effective because the seller perceives he is getting full value for his note.

N	%i	Pmt	PV	FV
180	.92	170.49	**15000**	0

Comment: This is the original note. You can offer to buy ⅓ of the payments now and ⅓ when 60 payments have been made and ⅓ when the last ⅓ of the payments will be made. In this case, you need to know the present value of ⅓ of the payments at your desired yield of 27%.

138.

⅓ of the payments is 60 N, at 27% yield.

N	%i	Pmt	PV	FV
60	27% ÷ 12	170.49	(?)	0

Comment: If you solve for **PV**, you will know what to pay for these payments.

139.

Answer: PV = $5,583. You will give the seller $5,583 now, $5,583 in 60 months, and $5,583 in 60 more months

BUY/SELL PROFIT: What if you sold the 60 payments to your 17% investor?

You change the **%i** to the investors yield of 17% and solve for **PV** to see what the investor would pay:

N	%i	Pmt	PV	FV
60	1.42	170.49	(?)	0

140.

Answer: PV = $6,860. Your investor will pay $6,860 for the right to receive 60 payments of $170.49. He should be willing to do the same thing again in 60 months and again 60 months after that.

Since you bought the 60 payments at a 27% yield or $5,583.35, and are selling them at a 17% yield or $6,860.05 your buy/sell profit is: $1,276.70

Summary:

You get: a commission of $1,276.70 and in 60 and
120 months you will get the same.

Seller gets: $5,583.35 Cash now and in 60 and
again in 120 months.

Seller's total cash is $5,583.35 times 3 equals:
$17,750. TOTAL CASH TO NOTE
SELLER FOR A $15,000 NOTE.

Investor gets: 60 payments of $170.49 for a 17% yield.
Cost: $6,860.05. Investor will do the same in
60 and 120 months.

You can see that fully amortizing loans offer several options to the discount note buyer and broker who has a clear grasp of how to use the financial calculator to his or her advantage. In the next note, involving balloon payments, even more options are available.

Note 2:

Calculating offers on an interest only note with a balloon payment

For our final *real world* example, we want to work with a note having a balloon payment due. Recently a note was presented to us. It was a large second with a present value of $160,000. The terms were interest only for 36 months at 12% interest with monthly payments of $1,600. There was obviously a balloon payment of $160,000 (remember with interest only the present value is never reduced over the life of the note). It is diagrammed as follows:

Original Loan

N	%i	Pmt	PV	FV
36	1	1600	160000	160000
				141.

It was a second note behind a $560,000 first. It was being created out of the purchase of a commercial building in a very nice section of San Francisco. The building had sold for $1,020,000 and, therefore, had a very decent Loan to Value of 71%. In calculating the offers we were going to make (we always try to give at least three offers), we realized that there were at least ten valid offers that could be made. As we thought about this note, we began to again think about all the factors that people consider in finally accepting the offer they do. Image now that this note is presented to you to make offers on (throughout you will work with a 20% return).

Things are more like they used to be than they are now.

Offer 1:

Offer to buy part of the payments

Original Loan

N	%i	Pmt	PV	FV
36	1	1600	160000	160000

142.

How much cash do they want or need NOW? If people do not have a specific purpose for a certain amount of money now, they may be nervous about having too much money at one time with no specific plan of what to do with it. Such people might want to sell just part of the note up to the amount they need. So let's look at different partial offers:

1). You could buy some of the payments, e.g., 20 payments, and the seller would then get the last 16 payments plus the balloon (You need a 20% return):

N	%i	Pmt	PV	FV
20	20 ÷ 12 = 1.67	1600	(?)	0

143.

Answer: PV = $27,023. Present the offer to the seller this way:

Summary:

Seller gets: $27,023.76 NOW plus $25,600 (16 payments of $1600) plus the balloon of $160,000 = TOTAL CASH: $212,623.76.

You get: 20 payments of $1,600 for a cost of $27,023 and a yield of 20% per year.

2). You can offer to purchase half of each payment. The seller would still receive $800 per month plus the balloon.

N	%i	Pmt	PV	FV
36	1.67	800	(?)	0

144.

Answer: PV = $21,526.

Summary:

Seller gets: $21,526 NOW plus $28,800 (36 payments of $800) plus the balloon of $160,000 = TOTAL CASH OF $210,326.

You get: 36 payments of $800 for a cost of $21,526 and a yield of 20% per year.

3). You could offer to buy half the balloon. The seller would then get cash now, monthly payments, plus some cash in 36 months:

N	%i	Pmt	PV	FV
36	1.67	0	(?)	80000 145.

Answer: **PV** = $44,122.

Summary:

Seller gets: $44,122 NOW plus $57,600 (36
    payments of $1600) plus half the balloon of
$80,000. TOTAL CASH OF $181,722.

You get: a balloon payment of $80,000 in 36
    months for a cost of $44,122 and a yield of
20% per year.

Offer 2:
Offer to buy the whole note

Original Loan

N	%i	Pmt	PV	FV
36	1	1600	160000	160000

146.

How nervous are the note holders about holding the note, waiting on monthly payments, and wondering if they will get the balloon when it is due? Such note sellers are eager to sell the whole note if they like the amount offered. How much can you purchase the whole note for at a 20% yield?

N	%i	Pmt	PV	FV
			(?)	

Comment: We're sure you can figure this one now that you know all the terms.

147.

Answer: PV = $131,298. That is also the total cash to the seller and you now own the whole note.

Offer 3:
Offer to buy just the balloon

Original Loan				
N	%i	Pmt	PV	FV
36	12	1600	160000	160000

148.

Some people want some cash NOW but like the idea of some extra money coming to them each month. They might be willing to sell just the balloon. How much would you pay for just the balloon payment at a 20% yield?

N	%i	Pmt	PV	FV
			(?)	

Comment: This is a chance to play with Future Value as it relates to Present Value. Remember you don't use payments at all and there is a big "0" under **Pmt**.

149.

Answer: **PV** = $88,245.

Summary:

Seller gets: $88,245.17 NOW $57,600 (all the payments) = TOTAL CASH OF $145,845.17.

You get: the $160,000 balloon in 36 months for a cost of $88,245 now for a 20% annual yield.

Offer 4:
Offer to buy just the payments

Original Loan N	%i	Pmt	PV	FV
36	12	1600	160000	160000
				150.

Some people don't want to worry about whether that check will arrive every month or not, but like the idea of a little "nest egg" of cash down the line. They might sell the payments only and want to keep the balloon for themselves.

1). You could purchase all the payments and none of the balloon. How much would you pay for the payments only at a 20% yield on the above note.

N	%i	Pmt	PV	FV
				(?)

Comment: Remember to put "0" under **FV** as you are only calculating the payments.

151.

Answer: PV = $43,053.

Summary:

Seller gets: $43,052.90 NOW plus the balloon of
$160,000 = TOTAL CASH OF $203,052.

You get: 36 payments of $1,600 for a cost of
$43,052 at an annual yield of 20%

2). You could purchase all the payments plus **part** of the balloon. Now this may seem a little more complicated, but it is really quite simple.

We want to make **20%** per year on our money. So we take the monthly payments and multiply them by twelve months.

Step # 1: $1600 (payments) x 12 = $19,200

This gives us our annual income from the note.

Now we must calculate how much to invest to receive that 20% yield. To do this we simply divide that annual income by our desired yield.

Step # 2: $19,200 divided by .20 (20%) = $96,000

This tells us that if we invest $96,000 and receive $19,200 per year (or $1,600 per month) we will be receiving 20% on our money each year. However, at some point we need to get back our original investment. In this case we will receive 20% per year (or 1.67% per month) for 3 years and then the **Seller** of the note must give us back our original investment of $96,000 out of the $160,000 balloon he will receive from the **Payor**:

N	%i	Pmt	PV	FV
36	1.67	1600	(?)	(?)
				152.

Answer: PV = $96,000 and **FV** = $96,000. The Present Value and Future Value are the same. You get back exactly what you gave to the seller and received 20% worth of payments on the Present Value of $96,000 for 36 months and then get your money back. **The seller receives the rest of the balloon or $64,000.**

Summary:

Seller gets: $96,000 NOW plus $64,000 when the
balloon is due = TOTAL CASH OF $160,000.
(The seller gets full amount of note.)

You get: 36 payments of $1600 and a balloon of
$96,000 in 36 months at a cost of $96,000 for a
yield of 20% per year.

Offer 5:

Offer to buy part of the payments and part of the balloon

Original Loan				
N	%i	Pmt	PV	FV
36	12	1600	160000	160000
				153.

Some want it all: some payments each month, a lump some of cash waiting for them in three years, but want some cash NOW as well. You could offer to buy half the payments and half the balloon for cash now.

N	%i	Pmt	PV	FV
36	1.67	800	(?)	80000
				154.

Answer: PV = $65,649.

Summary:

You get: the right to receive 36 payments of $800 and a balloon of $80,000 in 36 months at a cost of $65,649 for a yield of 20%.

Seller gets: $65,649.03 NOW plus $28,800 in payments ($800 x 36) plus $80,000 when the balloon is due = TOTAL CASH OF $174,449.03.

Offer 6:

Offer to buy half of note now, half later

Some sellers would like to sell the whole note and be done with it, but don't like the steep discount that's involved. For them, an offer of 100% of the present value but with flexible terms might be acceptable. Try offering half now and half in 36 months when the balloon is due.

N	%i	Pmt	PV	FV
36	(?)	1600	80000	80000

Comment: Since we are offering half now, we know the **PV** will be $80,000. We are offering the other half in 36 months. We know the **FV** will also be $80,000. So in this case we are solving for **%i**, not **PV**.

155.

Answer: **%i** = 24%. If you want an even better interest rate, you can offer 90% of **PV**: $160,000 - 10% = $144,000 (half is then $72,000 in **PV** and **FV**.) The answer is 26.67%. (As was shown in note #1, we could also offer to purchase the note in thirds: ⅓ NOW, ⅓ in 18 months, and ⅓ in 36 months when the balloon is due. See page 149.)

Wasn't that great seeing all the different possible offers available to you! Yet all these offers are just variations on using the Present Value and Future Value that you learned throughout this book. As you go along you will discover even more ways of purchasing a note. The point is that the more options you have available to you and the more sensitive you are to the needs of the seller, the better chance you have of meeting those needs, and thus getting the seller to accept one of your offers.

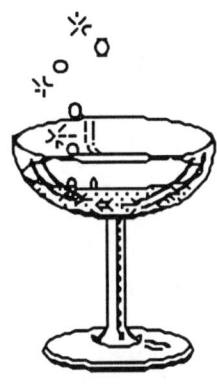

You are now ready to take your calculator and "attack" any note that is presented to you. Remember two or three offers are always better than one. The seller is choosing between this offer or that offer, rather than whether to take the one and only offer you have presented.

> **"It's no trick to make a lot of money, if all you want to do is make a lot of money."**
>
> **EVERETT SLOAN in *Citizen Kane***

Notes

Conclusion

In our introduction, we talked about developing an "infectious" enthusiasm for the calculator. We were rhapsodic about "dancing" over the keys as our financial calculator magically came up with the mathematically correct answers to our every situation. Did we exaggerate? Did we extol its virtues too highly? We don't think so! We are incorrigibly "hooked" on our calculators. If you have followed the lessons in this book conscientiously and carefully, then you also will begin to feel this delight in the capacities and possibilities of your financial calculator. Keep "playing" with it, keep using it, and we feel very confident that it will serve you very well. **You are now well on your way to success in your new note business!**

"There are no wrong notes."

THELONIOUS MONK

Appendix #1:

Common Errors

1. The most common error is not being consistent with time periods and interest rates. If the problem calls for monthly payments, the annual interest must be divided by 12 and the years must be multiplied by 12. If the problem asks for semi-annual payments you must divide the annual interest rate by 2 and you must multiply the years by 2.

2. The second most common error happens when entering the months and interest rates because you neglected to push the equal button. For example, to find the monthly interest of a 13% mortgage, the key sequence would be 13, ÷, 12, =, 1.08, **%i**.

3. Modern calculators have *constant memory.* If you turn them off the numbers you last used will remain in the financial registers. You must clear the calculator of everything in the memory before beginning a new problem.

4. Many calculators have more than one *mode.* Verify you are in the financial mode when doing financial calculations.

5. Many calculators have a convention that calls for money going out to be a negative number, and money coming in to be a positive number. Check your manual to see how you are to input these numbers.

6. Some calculators automatically divide the interest rate by 12, assuming you are asking for a monthly solution. If you are figuring an annual or other payment you must change the number of payments per year. Check your owner's manual for instructions.

Appendix #2:

Glossary

Amortized Loan: A loan that is completely paid off, interest and principal, by a series of regular payments that are equal or nearly equal.

Balloon Payment: Any payment on a loan that is more than twice the amount of the regular payment. A large payment on a regular payment loan.

Buy/Sell: The process of buying a note in your name and then selling it to someone else. This procedure is used when you do not want the investor or note seller to learn the amount of profit you are making.

First Loan: This loan was recorded first in the county recorder's office. If there is a foreclosure and sale, this loan will be paid first from the sale proceeds. Any money left will go to the Second Note holder.

Institutional Investor: A corporation or large company that invests in notes and who will buy from note brokers. They usually have very strict criteria for the notes they will buy, e.g., no second notes behind large first notes, low loan to value ratios, no land notes, etc.

Investor: A passive investor in notes. He or she buys the notes from note brokers at a yield somewhat higher than the prime bank lending rate. They are usually people who want safe investments in well-placed real estate.

Note Broker: A person who finds the seller of a note and links him or her to an investor in notes. The broker gets a commission for this service.

Note: This is the I. O. U. that explains the terms of the loan.

Second Loan: This loan was recorded second in the county recorder's office. It is a riskier loan than the First Loan. If there is not enough money left after paying the First Loan Holder after the foreclosure sale, the holder of the Second Loan may lose his or her money. This is also called a *Junior Loan*. There can also be a Third Loan and Fourth Loan.

Trust Deed: This document makes the property security for the loan. It is recorded at the County Recorder's Office and is sometimes incorrectly called a *mortgage*.

Underlying Loans: This refers to any loans senior to your loan. If you own a Fourth loan, the First, Second, and Third Loans are underlying loans.

Appendix #3:

Answers to QUESTIONS & CHALLENGES

Box #	N	ANNUAL %i	Pmt	PV	FV
1	360	10.00%	$877.57	($100,000)	$0
2	300	9.00%	*$1,678.39*	($200,000)	$0
3	12	5.00%	*$27.08*	($300)	$0
4	324	7.50%	*$38,504.89*	($5,342,456)	$0
5	13	15.50%	*$1,922.88*	($10,500)	$0
6	228	9.75%	*$53.07*	($5,500)	$0
7	80	13.75%	*$5,181.62*	($75,000)	$0
8	120	11.50%	$843.57	*($60,000)*	$0
9	115	11.50%	$843.57	*($58,631)*	$0
10	95	11.50%	$843.57	*($52,454)*	$0
11	1	11.50%	$843.57	($835.57)	$0
12	120	11.50%	$843.57	($60,000)	$0
13	5	11.50%	$843.57	($60,000)	*$58,631*
14	132	13.50%	$168.67	*($11,569)*	$0
15	12	13.50%	$168.75	($12,000)	*$11,569*
16	4	13.50%	$168.64	*($656)*	$0
17	140	13.50%	$168.69	($12,000)	*$656*
18	60	12.00%	*$500.00*	($50,000)	$50,000
19	60	12.00%	$30.00	($3,000)	*$3,000*
20	120	12.00%	$30.00	($3,000)	*$3,000*
21	10000	12.00%	$30.00	($3,000)	$3,000
22	360	14.50%	*$122.46*	($10,000)	$0
23	60	14.50%	$122.46	($10,000)	*$9,858*
24	3	12.00%	$4,754.05	($46,000)	*$48,584.62*
25	60	*13.94%*	$0.00	($100)	$200
26	60	7.00%	$0.00	*$7,129*	($10,000)
27	240	18.00%	$41,666.67	*($2,699,822)*	$0
28	20	18.00%	$0.00	*($10,951.69)*	$300,000
29	12	9.00%	$0.00	*($124,437.15)*	$350,000
30	144	9.00%	$0.00	($250,000)	*$733,209*
31	5	12.00%	$0.00	*($6,809.12)*	$12,000
32	35	20.00%	$0.00	*($1,693.00)*	$1,000,000
33	120	10.00%	$100.00	*($7,567)*	$0
34	360	10.00%	*$2,193.93*	($250,000)	$0
35	360	22.00%	$2,193.93	*($119,496.00)*	$0
36	240	11.00%	*$1,548.28*	($150,000)	$0
37	240	14.00%	$1,548.28	*($124,507.77)*	$0
38	240	12.00%	$1,548.28	($140,613.89)	$0
39	60	12.00%	$0.00	($100,000)	*$181,669.67*

Small differences in answers are due to "rounding errors" and are not significant.

Box #	N	ANNUAL %i	Pmt	PV	FV
40	60	7.00%	$0.00	$7,129	*($10,106.25)*
41	7	5.00%	$0.00	($350,000)	*$492,485.15*
42	12	7.00%	$0.00	($45,000)	*$101,348.62*
43	12	9.00%	$0.00	*($36,032.95)*	$101,348.62
44	1440	10.00%	$0.00	($25.00)	*$3,871,497.26*
45	62	25.00%	$0.00	($1.00)	*$1,019,578.82*
46	60	13.94%	$0.00	$5.00	*($10.00)*
47	36	5.50%	*($128.06)*	$0	$5,000
48	48	6.00%	*($184.85)*	$0	$10,000
49	*36*	6.00%	($254.22)	$0	$10,000
50	36	*21.55%*	($100.00)	$0	$5,000
51	12	7.00%	$0.00	($45,000)	*$101,348.62*
52	144	9.00%	*($393.26)*	$0	$101,349
53	240	20.00%	*($321.58)*	$0	$1,000,000
54	36	15.00%	*($775.79)*	$0	$35,000
55	180	12.00%	$240.03	($20,000)	$0
56	180	20.00%	$240.03	*($13,667)*	$0
57	120	18.00%	$143.46	*($7,962)*	$0
58	34	18.00%	($143.46)	*$3,799*	$0
59	84	12.00%	*$365.00*	($36,500)	$36,500
60	36	12.00%	$365.00	($36,500)	$36,500
61	36	*28.00%*	$365.00	*($24,734)*	$36,500
62	18	*21.95%*	$0.00	($70,000)	$97,000
63	72	10.00%	*$833.66*	($45,000)	$0
64	66	22.50%	$833.66	*($31,415)*	$0
65	*23*	22.50%	$833.66	($15,460)	$0
66	43	10.00%	$833.66	*($30,024)*	$0
67	29	10.00%	$833.66	($45,000)	$30,024
68	60	18.00%	($0.00)	*($20,465)*	$50,000
69	24	16.00%	($0.01)	*($10,915)*	$15,000
70	144	21.00%	$0.00	*($41,116)*	$500,000
71	12	15.00%	$0.00	*($17,230)*	$20,000
72	60	12.00%	*$450.00*	($45,000)	$45,000
73	60	19.50%	($450.00)	*$17,164.80*	$0
74	24	18.00%	$100.00	*($2,003)*	$0
75	120	23.00%	$1,999.99	*($93,655)*	$0
76	24	12.50%	*$364.58*	($35,000)	$35,000
77	24	31.00%	$364.53	($6,460)	$0
78	156	10.00%	*$401.75*	($35,000)	$0

Small differences in answers are due to "rounding errors" and are not significant.

Box #	N	ANNUAL %i	Pmt	PV	FV
79	156	31.00%	$401.73	($15,260)	$0
80	24	31.00%	$0.00	($8,274)	$15,260
81	60	21.75%	$1,000.00	($36,394)	$0
82	96	10.00%	$1,517.42	($100,000)	$0
83	96	21.75%	$1,517.41	($68,794)	$0
84	60	21.75%	$0.00	($23,414)	$68,794
85			PV=	$59,809	
86	36	18.00%	$762.81	($21,099.85)	$0
87	144	18.00%	$819.62	($48,237.92)	$0
88	36	18.00%	$0.00	($28,223.51)	$48,238
89			PV=	($49,323)	
90	360	13.00%	$165.93	($15,000)	$0
91	360	25.00%	$165.91	($7,959)	$0
92	60	25.00%	$165.92	($5,653)	$0
93	300	13.00%	$165.93	($14,712)	$0
94	360	13.00%	$165.93	($15,000)	$0
95	180	25.00%	$165.91	($7,769)	$0
96	180	25.00%	$0.00	($189.89)	$7,769
97	36	13.50%	$373.29	($11,000)	$0
98	18	28.00%	$373.29	($5,435.77)	$0
99	18	28.00%	$0.00	($3,588.83)	$5,436
100	18	13.50%	$373.23	($6,051)	$0
101	360	10.00%	$877.57	($100,000)	$0
102	9.38	19.00%	$577.57	($5,000)	$0
103	10	2.71%	$577.57	($5,000)	$0
104	60	32.00%	$250.00	($7,442)	$0
105	50	25.00%	$500.00	($15,440)	$0
106	11	20.00%	$1,000.00	($10,000)	$0
107	36	24.00%	($0.00)	($12,255.50)	$25,000
108	36	24.00%	$0.00	($18,000)	$36,717.90
109	60	18.00%	$0.00	($30,697.20)	$75,000
110	360	19.00%	$0.00	($1,749.38)	$500,000
111	360	10.00%	$877.57	($100,000)	$0
112	360	26.00%	$877.57	($40,485)	$0
113	180	26.00%	$877.56	($39,648)	$0
114	120	26.00%	$877.57	($37,410)	$0
115	180	27.00%	$568.30	($24,797)	$0
116	90	27.00%	$568.29	($21,848)	$0
117	45	27.00%	$568.30	($15,978)	$0

Small differences in answers are due to "rounding errors" and are not significant.

Box #	N	ANNUAL %i	Pmt	PV	FV
118	1	27.00%	$568.30	($556)	$0
119	$50,000.00	$15,000.00	$65,000.00	$75,000	86.67%
120	$50,000.00	$25,000.00	$75,000.00	$200,000	37.50%
121	$75,000.00	$35,000.00	$110,000.00	$150,000	73.33%
122	$123,456.00	$64,325.21	$187,781.21	$321,000	58.50%
123	60	10.00%	*$583.33*	($70,000)	$70,000
124	60	14.00%	$583.33	($59,972)	$70,000
125	240	10.00%	*($1,640.54)*	$170,000	$0
126	240	14.00%	$1,640.54	*($131,927)*	$0
127	180	11.00%	$170.49	($15,000)	$0
128	180	27.00%	$170.48	*($7,439)*	$0
129	180	17.00%	$170.48	*($11,077)*	$0
130	180	11.00%	$170.49	($15,000)	$0
131	90	27.00%	$170.48	*($6,554)*	$0
132	90	11.00%	$170.48	*($10,417)*	$0
133	90	17.00%	$170.49	*($8,642)*	$0
134	180	11.00%	$170.49	($15,000)	$0
135	180	27.00%	$85.23	*($3,719)*	$0
136	90	27.00%	$85.24	*($3,277)*	$0
137	90	17.00%	$85.25	($4,321)	$0
138	180	11.00%	$170.49	($15,000)	$0
139	60	27.00%	$170.48	*($5,583)*	$0
140	60	17.00%	$170.49	*($6,860)*	$0
141	36	12.00%	$1,600.00	($160,000)	$160,000
142	36	12.00%	$1,600.00	($160,000)	$160,000
143	20	20.00%	$1,600.00	*($27,024)*	$0
144	36	20.00%	($800.00)	$21,527	$0
145	36	20.00%	($0.00)	*($44,122)*	$80,000
146	36	12.00%	$1,600.00	*($160,000)*	$160,000
147	36	20.00%	$1,600.00	*($131,298)*	$160,000
148	36	12.00%	$1,600.00	*($160,000)*	$160,000
149	36	20.00%	($0.00)	*($88,245)*	$160,000
150	36	12.00%	$1,600.00	*($160,000)*	$160,000
151	36	20.00%	$1,600.00	*($43,053)*	$0
152	36	20.00%	$1,600.00	*($96,000)*	*$96,000*
153	36	12.00%	$1,600.00	($160,000)	$160,000
154	36	20.00%	$800.00	*($65,649)*	$80,000
155	36	*24.00%*	$1,600.00	($80,000)	$80,000

Small differences in answers are due to "rounding errors" and are not significant.

Free 3 month subscription to *NoteWorthy Newsletter,*

the major newsletter for the discounted note industry.
Mail this form to:

NoteWorthy Investments, Inc., P. O. Box 31451, San Francisco, CA 94131
OR
Fax this form to: (415) 824-7720.

• Send my free 3 months subscription to:

Name: _____

Company Name: _____

Address: _____

City: _____ State: _____ Zip: _____

Phone: (_____)_____

Fax Phone: (_____)_____

Where did you buy this book ?_____

Note*Worthy*
Discounted Note Catalog

❏ ONE YEAR SUBSCRIPTION TO **NOTEWORTHY**, the indispensable newsletter for Note Brokers, Buyers and Real Estate Investors. (Includes tape: **How To Find All The Notes You Could Ever Hope to Buy** and **NoteWorthy** list of 125+ institutional note buyers)..................... **$89/year**

BOOKS

❏ *CALCULATOR POWER!* BY **JON RICHARDS & DAVE ROBERTS.** This exciting book will help you develop the calculator expertise you need to make tremendous profits in the discounted note business. Learn how to make 45 offers on one cash flow. Dazzle your competitors. Includes a 3 month **Note-Worthy** subscription **$39.95**

❏ *SMART TRUST DEED INVESTING IN CALIFORNIA,* **BY GEORGE COATS** The best book written on trust deed investing. 90% of the information is relevant for all states. **$23.50**

❏ *THE COMPLETE GUIDE TO JUDGEMENT INVESTMENT* BY **MARK AND LLOYD WALTERS.** Its true! You can regularly buy judgements for 5 to 25 cents on the dollar. This book tells you exactly how to buy and collect. A big fat manual by those who have done it **$98.00**

❏ *HOW TO FIND ALL THE NOTES YOU COULD EVER HOPE TO BUY.* BY **LLOYD AND MARK WALTERS.**
Free brochure ideas, direct mail flyers, letters and much more. Feel free to copy and adapt the many ideas in this book. **$39.95**

❏ *DEALS ON WHEELS*: BY **LONNIE SCRUGGS.** How to buy, lease and finance used mobile homes for big profits. This book will teach you the little known business of financing used mobile homes for huge (60%) returns. **$23.50**

❏ *MAKING MONEY WITH MOBILE HOMES* BY **LONNIE SCRUGGS.** This fine follow-up book to **Deals On Wheels** shows you ways to make unbelievable profits and high yields in the Used Mobile home business **$23.50**

❏ *HOW TO START A DISCOUNTED NOTE BUSINESS: THE KIT.* BY **JON RICHARDS.** A book, two cassette tape, note buyer information, amortization computer program and more. Ideal start-up kit for the new note broker. Explains how a typical note business is structured and how you can start and run your own note business. **$65.00**

❏ *LORELEI'S LEGAL LESSONS: THE ESSENTIAL GUIDE FOR SUCCESSFUL NOTE BROKERS.* **BY LORELEI STEVENS.** By the president of **Wall Street Brokers**. This fine book explores legal and ethical ways to buy, broker and sell discounted notes. **$27.00**

❏ *OWNER WILL CARRY: HOW TO TAKE BACK A MORTGAGE WITHOUT BEING TAKEN.* **BY G. ROSENBERG & B. BROADBENT.** An insider's guide to seller carry back financing techniques that work all the time **$29.00**

COMPUTER SOFTWARE

❏ **DIRECT CONNECT, WIN95 OR 98**: Powerful data base of corporate cash flow buyers. Simply click a button and **Direct Connect** will update itself with the latest information. Helps you find and package your cash flows to the best corporate note buyers ($19 with **NoteWorthy** subscription) **$49.00**

❑ **NOTE QUOTER PRO, WIN95 OR 98:** Easy to use program gives you 27 different ways to buy a cash flow. Computes your profit, investor's yield, seller's cash and writes a purchase letter to the note seller. Very easy to use and very powerful. Never make a mistake again in your calculations. ***$129.00***

❑ **WORKING WITH REALTORS©, WIN95 OR 98: VIDEO, SOFTWARE, BOOKLETS & ADVERTISING.** This two hour video shows **Jon Richards** teaching a class to Realtors and includes explanations of the "Working With Realtors" approach. Kit includes postcards, flyers and ads to help you find Realtors to work with. The software gives you everything you need to create a note at the point of purchase. Input Seller's cash requirements, Buyer's Down Payment and Note Buyer's yield requirements. ***WWR*** will calculate several possible scenarios that meet each parties needs and will write a letter to the Realtor, Seller and Buyer explaining the terms of the sale. Easy to use (Software alone is $129)... .... ***$249.00***

❑ **NOTESMITH, WIN95 OR 98:** The very best accounting and report program for Note Buyers. Does 1098s and 1099s at year end, posts periodic payments and keeps track of your entire business. Pro and regular versions. An essential program for all note buyers. .... ***Pro $499.00; Plus $249.00***

❑ **NOTEWORKS: PC MACINTOSH SOFTWARE.** By the authors of **NoteSmith:** This program runs under ***Microsoft Works***. NoteWorks includes a complete electronic note buying office. Generates marketing letters, offer letters, work sheets, data bases, and spread sheets. Over 60 pages of letters, forms and works sheets compiled by professional note buyers. Very comprehensive program. Prices are for the Template only. You can buy **Microsoft Works** from your dealer or mail order. ***$160.00***

❑ **T-VALUE: PC** OR **MACINTOSH SOFTWARE.** This is the indispensable software program for anyone interested in the **time value of money,** the note business or investing. Use it for analyzing complex cash flows and generating very professional amortization schedules. ***$99.00***

TAPE CASSETTE PROGRAMS

❑ **PROFITS IN DISCOUNTED NOTES—THE COMPLETE BEGINNING COURSE**: Includes 18 hours of cassette instruction, a 700 page manual, all the contracts you need, over 126 ways to find notes, hundreds of marketing and advertising ideas and the latest list of institutional note buyers. This program has everything you need to start your discounted note business. Course includes support after the class. ***$495.00***

❑ **HOME STUDY COURSE BY HANK HARENBERG ON ADVANCED MARKETING & PROSPECTING TECHNIQUES:** The complete audio recording and notebook of Hank's intensive two-day class that concentrates on the specific techniques for cultivating professional business sources for the referral of numerous, undiscovered, untouched private owner financed real estate notes. ***$395.00***

❑ **THE AMAZING NOTE RECASTER KIT: JOHN BECK, JON RICHARDS, ISTVÁN SIPOSS.** Everything you need to "improve" a note by changing the terms for the benefit of the payor. Kit contains powerful Win 95 Software to calculate an infinite number of ways to change the terms of the note to increase its yield. Kit contains cassette tapes and all the documentation and contracts you need to make your notes much more valuable. ***$129.00***

Total Order	$_____
Shipping & Handling: ($4.00 First item, $2 each additional item)	$_____
CA Residents Add 8.5% Tax:	$_____
TOTAL ENCLOSED:	$_____
Today's Date:	_____ 20_____

Send Check or Cash or Money Order To: NoteWorthy, P. O. Box 31451, San Francisco, CA 94131
OR: Call 1(800) 487-1864 to charge by phone.

Name: _____
Address: _____
City:_____ State:_____ Zip:_____
Phone: (_____)_____ Fax: (____)_____
Credit Card:_____Exp:_____

Or: Fax This Form to: (415) 824-7720
For more products and information visit our secure on-line store at:
www.noteworthyusa.com